POETRY NOW

WALES 1997

Edited by Andrew Head

First published in Great Britain in 1997 by
POETRY NOW
1-2 Wainman Road, Woodston,
Peterborough, PE2 7BU

All Rights Reserved

Copyright Contributors 1996

HB ISBN 1 86188 515 6
SB ISBN 1 86188 510 5

FOREWORD

Although we are a nation of poetry writers we are accused of not reading poetry and not buying poetry books: after many years of listening to the incessant gripes of poetry publishers, I can only assume that the books they publish, in general, are books that most people do not want to read.

Poetry should not be obscure, introverted, and as cryptic as a crossword puzzle: it is the poet's duty to reach out and embrace the world.

The world owes the poet nothing and we should not be expected to dig and delve into a rambling discourse searching for some inner meaning.

The reason we write poetry (and almost all of us do) is because we want to communicate: an ideal; an idea; or a specific feeling. Poetry is as essential in communication, as a letter; a radio; a telephone, and the main criteria for selecting the poems in this anthology is very simple: they communicate.

Faced with hundreds of poems and a limited amount of space, the task of choosing the final poems was difficult and as editor one tries to be as detached as possible (quite often editors can become a barrier in the writer-reader exchange) acting as go between, making the connection, not censoring because of personal taste.

'In every volume of poems something good may be found'

(Samuel Johnson)

In a world with many social and political issues we all have our own opinions. But with so many contrasting views, it is often difficult to get our voice heard.

Perhaps one of the most successful ways to communicate is through poetry, where the poets can be honest and truthful without the interference of a difference in opinion.

Poetry Now Wales 1997 has brought together the voices of today's generation in a collection of poetry which communicates directly with the reader.

The poems vary in form and style, some modern, some traditional. The themes also vary, including love, war, death, people and politics which have moved poets throughout the ages.

This anthology represents the up and coming poets of Wales and the issues that inspire their poetry.

The success of this collection, and all previous *Poetry Now* anthologies, relies on the fact that there are as many individual readers as there are writers.

CONTENTS

Title	Author	Page
Skin	Jane Davies	1
Man Shadow	Christopher John Brock	2
The Dance	Carol Rickard	2
Hiding The Dragon	John Roughton	3
How Do You Mend A Broken Heart?	June Wood	4
The Fearless Stone	Jill Pritchard	4
Mother Toast	Christine William	5
Pensive Moments	M D Poyner	6
Untitled	J Wilson	6
Invisible Life?	Gwen Kirwan	7
My Mate At The Market	Leighton Haigh Edwards	8
Victim	Dorothy Neil	9
The Oak In The Wind	Ceri Nicholas	9
Love	Jean Howells	10
Debut	Rebecca Williams	10
To A Friend	Kate Evans	11
A Prayer For Peace	Christine Day	11
Black Gold	Rosemarie John	12
Davey's Journey	Patricia Tobin	12
The First World War	James Dyer	13
Dreams	Kara Tobin	14
For All The Golden Cats	A Bellamy	14
The School Rule	R Miles	15
Reflections	Valerie Baker Hughes	16
Daybreak	Denise Jones	16
The Gwili Railway	Yvonne Watkin-Rees	17
The Case Of Madam Butterfly	Richard O'neill	18
500 Miles On The Day	S A Dyer	19
Is It Time	V Miles	20
The Disappearing Valleys	M L Webb	21
The Relay Race	Maurice Chambers	22
Who Am I?	Irene E Rowlands	22
A Ray Of Hope	M Jones	23

Enemy	Ross I Standring	23
A Tribute To The Anonymous Graves	Gerard Phillips	24
Stephen	F Kettle	24
Reunion	John Thomas Jones	25
Wales	Diane Antoniazzi	26
Age Of Wonder	B E Eyre	26
Watching The World Go By	Richard W Finlan	27
So Precious	Terri Brant	28
The Tragedy Of Dunblane	Geraint Rhys Leach	28
Traffic Light Kids	S J Evans	29
Love Is . . .	Russell Charles Franklin	29
He's Mine	Elaine Marshall	30
Holiday Time	June Christensen	30
My Granddaughter	M Y Briggs	31
The Bully	Catherine Page	32
Flames	G Jones	33
Bill	Sylvia Currey	34
Aftermath	Doreen Davies-Paton	35
Inspirations	Y King	36
An Eagle	John Gilchrist	36
Crumlin Viaduct	Helen Rees-Smith	37
Saved	Samantha Cowlin	38
Untitled	Christine Lyons	39
Nan	Lyn Maureen Jones	40
Nightmare	M E O'Brien	41
Frosty Flakes	Rhys Oliver Hodge	41
The Lesson	Kay S Dunn	42
Castles	Paula Favorido	42
That Other World	K Lapham	43
Village Life	Joanne Griffiths & Thomas Griffiths	44
The Bomb	Claire M Bellamy	44
Stolen Moments	Anne Valeria Davies	45
Forgotten Dreams	Venetia Hogben	45
Racism	Sian Matthews	46

Bad Times	Andrew Byard	46
My Personal Storm	Linda Roberts	47
I Think It's Time	V Topp	48
Time Share	Gillian Avis	48
Shadows	Barry Townsend	49
This That I Don't Understand	M S Drabble	50
Our Nurses	W James	51
The Sea	James Channing	52
The Wales I Know	Marc A C Redman	52
Picasso's Pigeons	Jacqueline Jones	53
Life Saver	C Fisher	53
Stolen Lullaby	Phyllis Blue	54
Post Modernist Poet In Wales Maps	Paul Faulkner	55
Untitled	Rae Jones	56
The Sea Empress	Lynda Byard	56
Christmas Lament	Maureen Nixon	57
Postcards From Bevvy	Beverley Elliott	58
An Englishman Abroad (In Wales)	June Lane	59
Always The Trees (In Cwm Dyli)	Derek Mayes	60
A Gypsy Request	Peter Kuck	60
Steel Strike	Ralph May	61
Untitled	Brian Cox	62
Hope	Rhian W Roberts	62
The Flight Of The Crystal Gypsy	Mick Maddiver	63
Summer	M Hodges	64
The Thinker	Rhoda Lewis	64
The Ebony Tree	Jane Hunt	65
Homeless	Katie Williams	65
Kitchen Magic	B Holland	66
Simon's Soliloquy	Carole Weeks	67
Bird In July	Hywel Davies	68
Dreams	Louise Ghosh	68

Title	Author	Page
Mix-Up At Computer Dating Agency	Vivienne Bainton	69
The Greatest Story In The World	Gareth Jonn Owens	70
The Silver Moon	Michelle Beth Thomas	71
Visions Of The Nile	Mari-Clare Pearman	71
Still	R Phillips	72
Shipwreck	George R Green	72
A Fallen Man	Elizabeth Leach	73
Parting	K C Howells	74
Friends	Carl Hobbs	75
A Garden Of Music	Godfrey Martin	76
From A Newport Bar-Room	Steve Andrews	77
Animals	K M E Evans	77
Elegy For A Very Ordinary Cat	Leila Maryat	78
My Grandad	Liz Martin	78
There, They're, Their	Barbara Beaumont	79
Sir Galahad	Christine Williams	80
Jump	Gail Cureton	80
Live Longer Say No!	Joan Watkins	81
For Nan	Carol Mogford	81
Stranger In A Strange Land	Denise Pritchard	82
The Monmouthshire Brecon Canal . . .	Anne Whitcombe Sterry	83
Their Life	Alison Pearce	84
Reclamation	Larry Bowen	84
The Silver Stream	W H Williams	85
Buzzard	Richard Ball	86
Rosie	M B Chaplin	87
Hunt	Peter Hall	88
Margaret's Garden	J Roberts	89
Innocence Of Dunblane	Catherine Wallace	89
Banished	Ruth Curtis	90
What Is A Smile?	A J Luke	90
Romantic Rendezvous	Helen F Jones	91

Victoria	Catherine M Rees	92
Aegina Muse	Skelly	92
In Absentia	E R Kermode	93
Solitude	Lucy Vincent	94
Springtime	Gemma Ball	94
Bitter Hour	Elaine Hawkins	95
The Uncapped Gown	Carole Smith	96
Untitled	Tanya Louise Richard	96
I Can See You	Tiffany Aubrey	97
Resolution For The Millennium	Audrey Forbes-Handley	98
Anger	Judith Aubrey	98
Kite	Greta Maclean Jones	99
This Is It	Sue Smith	99
Yes Wales Is A Beautiful Place	E M Boyle	100
Days	C Wiles	101
Help Save The Animals	Kirsty Davies	101
Red As A Rose	Lianne Futia	102
The Love Spoon	Laura Föst	102
Weather In Wales	Anita Ghosh	103
Idle Gossip	Helen Deborah Bennett	104
Roses Round The Door	Marjorie Scott	105
Silent Lover	Claire Lovell	105
Small	Richard Reid	106
Perfect	M Pickering	106
Tears Of Love	Josephine Bottino	107
Very Like Ogden Nash	G Jones	107
Living On A Grant Cheque	Julie A Kinnair	108
Down A Hardened Rut	The Warwickshire Poet	109
The Eagle	Dafydd Williams	110
The Prisoner	Garnet Hoddell	110
Save Not Kill	Jayne Pearce	111
Bluebells	Anna Jackson-Scott	111
Long Summer Days	Audrey Adsett	112
The Storm	Diana Jackett	112
1966	David Sheppard	113

Title	Author	Page
I Do Believe	C Sumner	114
Look Around	Lucy Hartley	115
This Child Of Mine	Marcia Bailey	115
Turning Tides	Phil Williams	116
Access Day	E V	116
My Seaside Day	Laura Anne Evans	117
The Motorbike	K R Lamprey	117
Gratitude	Windsor Hopkins	118
The Cause	L A Churchill	119
Eco Warriors	Bob Lewis	119
At The Station	Kathleen Wendy Jones	120
Daybreak	Eileen Hollins	121
Luxury	Darren Snaith	121
The Fury Of Nature	Inas Everett	122
The Door	K Grady	122
My Taid	Claire Thomas	123
Spring	Sian Boissevain	124
Personal Fix	Janet Dalmar	124
The Sad Mountains	Kevin Bratherton	125
Sometimes	Keri L Thomas	126
And Did Those Feet?	P J Davies	127
Colouring My County	Frances Griffiths	128
Tempus Fugit	R Roberts	129
Our Fair Land	Dawn Ridler	130
Land O'Spirits	R Maskill	130
Summer A Walk At Dusk	Jacquie Williams	131
Tears Of Love	David Thomas	132
Street Vendor's Hyperbole	Douglas M Henly	132
The Caller At The Old Inn's Door	Norman Royal	133
Ambition	David Wederell	134
Time	Anne Jones	134
And Tell Me	Colin Davies	135
Why?	C A Edwards	136
Bosnia (The Blue Berets)	Middy	137
The Lonely Old Man	Natalie Bennett	138
Down In The Dell	Geraldine Ward	138

Reality	Claire Taylor	139
Decision	Debra Greenhouse	139
Man's Best Friend	Laurence Mann	140
Physically Measurable	Karen Newsham	141
Rain	Leighton Haigh Edwards	141
Who Needs Love?	Deborah C Jones	142
Progress	Shirley Silman	143
The Swing	Pauline Davies	144
Now	Susan Green	144
The Storm	Dariann Sealby	145
Blind, Deaf And Exceptionally Dumb!	Sylvia Pollard	145
My Sporting Son	Pauline Hickey	146
The Lost Poem	Zoë Pearce	147
Virtual Reality	Joan R Gilmour	147
Black Mountain White	Sylvia Shields	148
God's Garden	Eric Hope	149
A Christmas Message	Peter J Dewhurst	150
So In Love With You	Kate Jones	151
No Chance	Patricia Ann Evans	152
My Love	Chris Hassell	152
Ringing The Memory	Carolyn J Bartlett	153
The Artist	Lee W G T Morgan	153
Summer Hibernation	Sandra Lloyd-Jones	154
The Sun	Sophie Bennett	155
The Robin	Gladys Locke	156
The Dietician	J Owen	157
Countryside Cures	Sapphire Zagni	158
Redec Of Keiron	Janet Smith	159
Every Memory	S Meredith	160
Chopper	David Robinson	160
Peace	Thomas Lynch	161
Home Again	J P Williams	162
Fields Of Tranquillity	A R Rankin	162
Home	David Paul Lloyd	163
Starlings	Marilyn Gunn	164
Dolorous	A E Graham	165

The Snow And You	James Bull	166
Let It Be Soon	Yvonne Edwards	166
Soldier Boy	Marie Graha	167
My Boss	Veronica Summers	168
Spaceman	Winifred Jenkins	168
Miror, Mirror	James Sherman	169
Surviving	Dianne Brown	169
Tinkers	Tony Jennett	170
Cardiff	Terri Brant	171
Please Miss	James Thomas Hopkins	172
A Cry For Love	Janet Marian Burns	173
The Awakening	Our Bri	174
Coming Home	Pamela Williams	174
Brother	J E Hill	175
To A Slug	Maxwell Bruce	176
A Day In The Life Of Mr Mellow Ingram	Aled Hughes	177
Jack Frost	K King	178
Men Must Not Cry	Thomas Phelps	178
February	Sylvia Bevan	179
Evaluating Envy	Joy Marles-Roberts	180
Valley Of A Thousand Stars	Monica Mary Jackson	180
Life Jacket	Susan Richardson	181
They Didn't Understand Us	Tracy Wheeler	182
	Sonia Ruckley	183
Chocolate Cake	Karen Taylor	184
Green Grass	Mags Middleton	184
Variegation	Jane Cook	185
Secret As The Pollen	Angela Morton	185
Toy Soldier	Karren D Kinsey	186
Manhattan's Legacy	Ceri Vale	187
The Great Mystery	Rhiannon F Hart	188
Covetousness	Peter Gledhill	189
Creature Comforts	Margaret Cave	190
Emptiness	J Hatton	190
Joking Apart	Sue Whiting	191
My Baby Boy	K Brown	192

The British Legion Outing	Jane Wallis Hicks	193
Breathing Last Of		
The Once Made . . .	P J Thomas	194
Frustrated Psychopaths	Graham Griffiths	195
Wonderful	M J Kavanagh	196
Bubbles	Sue Davidson	197
The Simple Things	Ken Bruford	198
Site For Development	Andrew Hodson	199
Sonnet Of Sleepers	Sarah Jane Davies	199
Now, Of A Summer Evening	Andrew Sumner	200
After All	G Headley	201

SKIN

A thin flexible covering
sealing in
Tissue, sinew, bone
And the blue green veins
Threading together, bulging
Thick liquid, throbbing slowly
Back up pipes and tubes.

Babies' skin
Creamy milk white, talcum powdered,
Handle with care layer,
Smoothly covering
Tiny plump limbs
Dimpling at fingers, toes, cheeks,
Rose petal perfect.

Skin on my grandmother's hands,
Cling film thin,
Not so much a covering
As a window on her frailty
Succumbing
To a lifetime's weathering.

My skin
Hiding and protecting
While I, careless
Lived inside,
Seems to have become
Looser lately
And bruises rather easily.

Jane Davies

MAN SHADOW

Who were you man shadow that I long to know
Who lost his life so long ago.
Who were you who gave me life, yet lost his own.
Who were you in my field of dreams
Who gave me smiles in misty dreams of childhood.
Who were you who left my life an open wound
    through no fault of your own
A wound which still bleeds tears for you the one I long to know
You have left a vacuum of sad deep space I cannot fill
Who were you man shadow? I long to know.

Christopher John Brock

THE DANCE

The house creaks
The wind sighs
A pool of midnight black
Surrounds the wayward rocks
Where shadows
Fragile as gossamer
Move in the jagged circle.
Slowly begins the dance
Forms sinuous lines of intricate ritual
Until transported with delight
In whirling ecstasy
And self fulfilled
They pause and gaze in awe at what has come
A central focus for those shimmering shades.
But who or what is there
Cannot be seen by mortal eye
I turn rejected and alone
The creaking house my refuge
The sighing wind my cry.

Carol Rickard

HIDING THE DRAGON

Spruce now caps bold hills
And tourists pass an unnatural view
With their cars and caravans
For a site by the sea.
Pity them rushing, never knowing
Flights of hawks upon the thermals
Or native woodland paths
Where stunning silence laps around.

Quick down to the end of the river's run
Past all the secrets glances miss
With just a stop for a camera shot
Of castle walls, of dams, of quarries
Laid along the tarmac roads.

Battles, sieges, valleys flooded,
Slate and lead for roofs and wealth abroad,
An exodus to better things unknown -
These many secrets here and still a whisper
Of the songs the village music-makers raise
And pale-skinned Rachels use
To charm the sons of Owain.

Hurry, hurry by
For the pleasure of the sands
While this timber darkening
Takes its harvest from the hills
And the dragons of this country breathe a sigh.

John Roughton

HOW DO YOU MEND A BROKEN HEART?

How do you mend a broken heart
What do you say, where do you start
What can you do to build up their trust
Say something special, is surely a must

Show them the way to take the right road.
Carry their burdens and lighten their load,
but you can only do this for so long
for sooner or later they have to be strong

Whether grieving for loved ones
or a relationship split
there's no reasoning with you
for reasons don't fit.

Just pick yourself up, and brush yourself down
We'll go for a drink, a night on the town.
We'll have a good time, chase your troubles away
don't ponder on dreams of Yesterday

Time is a great healer, so they all say,
Life gets a little easier with each passing day
So keep your chin up, don't look to the ground.
Soon a smile will tell us of the new life you have found.

June Wood

THE FEARLESS STONE

Sometimes when I feel lonely,
When I feel afraid and unsure,
I wish that I could be strong and carefree
Like a tree, or the wind.

The wind holds no fears,
It doesn't feel pain
It can't be seen by the human eye.
Can God see the wind?

No, God cannot see the wind,
God can only hear the wind,
Feel the wind and like the wind,
And sometimes, fear the wind.

God can only experience the wind as we do.
Because God is inside us,
And sees and feels as we do.
Sometimes God doesn't know the wind exists,
When he is inside a stone.

Jill Pritchard

MOTHER TOAST

They call me mother toast
And shall I tell you why
I don't have a decent living
I hardly ever smile
My husband isn't working
Not money coming through
      The door
I try to put a brave face on
But I can't take it anymore

I blame this selfish government
17 years of Tory rule
My children wouldn't be eating much
If it wasn't for meals at school
And when we're all there in the
      Evening
I try to make something for tea
It's a little bit of what we have
And a piece of toast for me.

Christine Williams

PENSIVE MOMENTS

The sky looks stormy, so full of rain,
Shall we see sunshine soon again,
Birds are flitting amongst the trees,
Leaves are rustling in the cool strong breeze.

Bees are busy amongst the flowers,
distributing pollen through the daylight hours,
The moon has risen and shines so bright
catches the owl on its soundless flight.

Not everything slumbers through the hours of night,
the rustle of creatures goes on till light
of the sun's rays tinges the skies,
and the edges of darkness fades away and dies.

Once more the world springs into life
when the flowers re-open, and the air is spiced
with perfume so fragrant, and oh so bright
they create such beauty that brings delight.

The hearts of all, whose lonely hours
are spent remembering birds and flowers,
and sun, and moon, sunshine or rain
will life ever be quite the same again!

M D Poyner

UNTITLED

The silent leaves of summer burst into a
deafening whisper
At the first gentle caress of an autumn breeze
Why do they embrace their executioner so?
Is it really something that we don't know?
Or have they found the truth that we cannot
see,
Buried by years of doubt and fear?

Oh mother nature rise up again,
Awaken dormant hopes
And with your gentle touch,
remover the dust from sleeping eyes
That they may rejoice in the glory you bare
And feel no remorse for days gone by,
But share your joy in the birth of today.

J Wilson

INVISIBLE LIFE?

Praying it wouldn't rain again,
the girl sat quietly
amongst her home.

When she looked around,
no-one looked back.
Eyes averted quickly
when they glanced her way.

Her jumper was damp
and the night was creeping in.
If they didn't give soon
it would be too late.
A cup of tea was something to die for.

But not today.

The clink took her by surprise,
and looking up, she saw no-one.
In her tin was a whole pound coin.

She smiled
and quietly lay down
in her cardboard bed.
Praying it wouldn't rain again.

Gwen Kirwan

MY MATE AT THE MARKET

When I went down to the
Market, to buy myself some
Fish, they offered me a
Bloater, I said 'Darling you
Must be a joker, I'll have half
A pound of salt fish.'

The next week I went to the
Market they offered me a
Lemon sole, I told them
Quite politely 'You know I'm
Still on the dole, I'll
Have a pint of cockles
And make the best with that,
See you next week mate
We'll have a chat.'

The following week I had
Jellied eels, For I am far
Too young to have meals on
Wheels, He said 'How's your
Luck,' I said 'It's right out,'
'Never mind have this trout,
That's what mates are all
About,' 'Thank you for this
Treat, I'll see you next week.'

Leighton Haigh Edwards

VICTIM

I am a leaf, adrift on the breeze,
Torn asunder from the trees;
Spinning and whirling into the night,
Anxiously seeking dawn's faint light;
Helplessly sweeping, whisking away,
Venturing into light of day;
Thorns and branches, claws and darts,
Ripping, tearing me apart;
Snow and frost will I endure,
Rain and hail for ever more;
Tossed and buffeted around,
Soon to powder I am ground;
Blown, and blown, unceasingly,
Far into eternity.

Dorothy Neil

THE OAK IN THE WIND

The wind roars as it rushes towards the
                                      oak tree,
not a moment of silence as the sleeping
                                    people wake,
leaves crunching,
branches breaking.
The falling rain flows towards the river,
silently - the wind softly settles,
suddenly a cracking banging noise,
the oak falls and the wind blows away.
Now all is silent; no wind, no tree,
as the morning sun rises . . . silence is
everywhere.

Ceri Nicholas (14)

LOVE

Love is precious
We all need a lot.
On high days and low days
Just think what you've got
Cos when you are down
And things seem too bad
Just think of the good times
And what you have had.
It may buck you up
But whether or not
Just remember that with love
You will survive the lot.

Jean Howells

DEBUT

Twinkling like a noon star she shuffles in her brushed suedette shoes,
unsure of the slight heel.
Face caked, *like a clown* she thinks,
in rouge and with blue iridescent eyes.
Cherry lips painted a deeper scarlet,
Blonde locks held in a vice-like grip.
Itchy, unfamiliar dress rests low on her shoulders.
She presses herself to the heavy velvet wall,
bites a rose pink nail, then another, another.
She imagines how the raven and ivory will feel,
how the blazing lights will melt her icy exterior.
Sanctimonious harmonies fill her mind and
how suddenly she longs to turn and run!
A firm male hand grips her shoulder to rip her from her velvet refuge.
She stumbles towards either floor-pounding applause
or stony, stifled and embarrassed coughs . . .

She takes a deep breath.

Rebecca Williams

TO A FRIEND

I know that sometimes life is hard
It's not very often that we get dealt the winning card
But one must learn to play the game
To keep an even keel
And not let oneself be drowned by however one may feel.
This applies to all the things
The good as well as bad
For one can never be too happy and one can never be too sad.
So take a step back, go within
And search for the light inside
Nurture it, love it, let it shine, and don't ever let it hide.

Kate Evans

A PRAYER FOR PEACE

As the sun sets in the west
and the beasts lay down to rest.
Hunger and pain, sorrow no gain
as we have to move before the rain.
On and on up into the hills,
there is nowhere else for us to go.
Striving to feed our young and old,
as the white man moves us on for gold.
He takes over the land and buffalo.
We are now few in numbers, our spirits
are low. We are moved on to where the
grass does not grow. Where there is
little warmth from the snow.
Now there are just a few of us left
and we hope our culture will grow,
as we are moved to and fro.

Christine Day

BLACK GOLD

Far from the stumbling, solemn valleys
That once witnessed the destruction
Of its sinewy servants
Imprisoned in the tombs below Rhondda,
Men who sacrificed their breath
For the masters and dons of greed.
We watch in silence another carnage,
Rape of the craggy, wind-worshipped coast,
It's anarchist welcome to the wild sea
Stopped by newer sultans of wealth.
A thick, liquid gloom
Gaining possession of every sea-sculpted form,
Securing without protest, a realm
Rich with the noisy litany
Of creatures, whose salty wings
And roguish mariners eye
Swept across their golden shores of paradise.
Clothed now in funeral black
They lie in state,
Glistening like trinkets,
Offerings to the fat-bellied god of Mammon.

Rosemarie John

DAVEY'S JOURNEY

The shadow walks across the land,
Through frightened trees and stunted earth,
A pale echo now; of what was grand
No sign of joy, no sign of mirth.
Still Davey walks the hallowed land.

A miner once, so tall and strong,
From school to pit, he knew no other,
Though work was hard; a happy throng
Worked together, alongside friend and brother,
They always tried to get along.

It started well, that fateful day
Davey rose early, kissed his wife,
Kissed his children; that was his way,
No cares today, no worry or strife,
That Friday morning, twelfth of May.

The sirens screamed, the village froze,
The women wept, the children cried,
The village rallied, no one knows
How many trapped, how many died
Davey still walks because Davey knows.

Patricia Tobin

THE FIRST WORLD WAR

What is this life if full of war.
But dreams are only dreams.
And time is now and all we have is war
And I fear I shall be all alone.
When I get towards the end.

I wonder if you miss me sometimes.
When the *sunset turns to gold.*
My heart is with you, tonight my love.
As in the shadows your dearest face I see.
And I wonder if the girl I'm thinking of will sometimes
                              think of me.
O dry those tears my love.
For there's sunshine after rain.

I fancy I hear you calling me.
To my old home in Wales.
Say good-night but not good-bye.
And keep the home fires burning bright.
Till all the boys come home to Wales again.
And one day war will be no more.

James Dyer

DREAMS

I sit, I watch the scarlet sky,
It drifts above me as I start to sigh,
Off into my dream world as reality drifts by,
Oh why do I dream, oh why, oh why.

The meadows so lucious and green,
The most dreamy place I have ever seen,
The world that has never been,
To forget life, my mind seems so keen,
After all, it is the mind that brings the Dream.

Yet I walk through my world,
The future being unfurled,
In trees squirrels are curled.

Up in their dreamland faraway,
Maybe I'll see it another day.

Life is a mystery like a quiz,
You have to be alert just to live.

I sit, I watch the scarlet sky,
It drifts over me as I start to sigh,
Oh why, do I dream oh why, oh why.

Kara Tobin

FOR ALL THE GOLDEN CATS

Every night the golden cats
Come out to play.
Slip into their shimmering, sparkling coats
Golden haloes framing
Golden smiling faces.

Darting from the steely shadows
Prancing beneath the moonlight's austere glare
Phantoms of the dark.

Golden because they no longer live
At least not in our sphere
They exist as blithe spirits
Casualties of modern life
Their other selves lie splattered on the tarmac.

A Bellamy

THE SCHOOL RULE

The school rule,
Is don't be a fool,
Get on with your work,
And don't act cool.

Keep your head down,
Don't ask questions,
I'll write on the board,
You can copy the rest down.

Don't you get it,
Don't be so dull,
You should understand this,
Just like the rest of them.

Sit in the corner,
Sit on your own,
I can't be bothered with you,
Just leave me alone.

If you've got a problem,
Sort it out after school,
It's not up to me,
'Cause that's the school rule,
What's the problem,
I'm sorry the bell's rang
There's no time left, it's home time,
And that's my time.

R Miles

REFLECTIONS

A busy day in Ebbw Vale
Where men sit down and talk all day
Passing comments on ladies' skirts
Cor that's a bit high lads don't you think
As they all pass on a knowing wink.
Chitting and chatting about this and that
Anything to make the time go fast.
These are idle men you might think
With nothing to do all day but smoke and
Drink, but you I know different you
See with the steel-works closed and
The mines shut down our hearts go out
To those men in town.
Our kids grow up and move away
Because they're told no jobs today.

Valerie Baker Hughes

DAYBREAK

Softly you stole into my chamber
sparkling a thousand fires bright
with your smiling morning embrace.
Pale golden light and roseate hues,
ever tranquil and serene;
Adamantine dewdrops glistening
in the silvery dawn;
Diminishing stars -
eclipsed by your approach.
Rousing me from slumber with warm caresses
and sweet kisses bestowed upon my brow;
emitting glorious beams;
a blazing jewel in sky's blue looking glass;
the sun arose up in the east.

Denise Jones

THE GWILI RAILWAY

Time Past
The gleaming 'giant' on its tracks,
With shaking luggage on its racks;

A footplate strong, and shining brass,
Polished wood and gleaming glass;

Plushy seats and a sliding door,
There was no carpet on the floor;

Water-closets so often flushed,
Many corridors people-crushed;

Seaside views above some heads,
Several passengers in their beds;

Liveried men in brown and gold,
In temperatures both warm and cold,

Offering meals and many a drink
While knives and forks did gently clink;

And wartime-troops on their way to battle
As the train it rocked with swerve and rattle.

Time Present
How lovingly they tend with care
the steel-clad engine standing there.

With hammer and tools they strike with strength
Along the 'giant's' total length,

Restoring it for all to see
By the banks of River Gwili.

It makes its journeys many a day
Through a delightful woodland way,

Where stately foxgloves grow around
In ferns and grass upon the ground.

The puffing smoke and whistle shrill
Are heard along the sloping hill,

When passengers both old and young
Enjoy their journey full of fun,

Admiring in hours of leisure
Work that's done on all this 'treasure'.

Yvonne Watkin-Rees

THE CASE OF MADAM BUTTERFLY

It's a sight so balletic,
To watch her ride on the breeze,
Weaving through the daisies,
While feeling the bees' knees.

Adorned with natural colours,
No artist could have done,
In her translucent splendour,
She basks in the mid-day sun,
Until harassed by naughty children
Who will have her on the run.

Then from a well-kept garden,
Where death is delivered today,
Staggers this object of wonder
In her death-dive towards the clay.

No more will she paint the landscape,
With splashes of herself.
She is now confined for eternity
To a glass frame on the shelf.

Richard O'neill

500 MILES ON THE DAY

Birds up at 6.00 am, Dai,
Thurso so far away, Jim,
All they can do is but hope and pray,
That blazing red is home on the day.

No-one knows what lies ahead,
Farewell, Old Scotland; Carlisle, here I come.
The clouds up above have all turned to grey.
For the third time today.
Fly on Blazing Red, past Blackpool tower,
Keep thinking of home and Wales.
Blazing Red, it's where your father was born,
North Wales deep valleys, high mountains,
Green fields and rushing fountains.

The day is done and fades away,
Upon the silent moors of Hay,
The blackbird sings his goodnight song.
Fly on blazing red fly on.
The Breacon beacons are very high,
They nearly reach up to the sky.
Is that Aberdare?
Not long now, blazing red.
Come on down to the Rhondda and Fern Dale.
You're nearly home Blazing Red.

Wake up, Jim what's that up in the sky, Dai?
It's Blazing Red.
I only hope it is, no doubt about it.
He's on the loft and now in the clock
He stands alone and so proud.
He's the only bird home on the day.

That's *Jim's Blazing Red.*

S A Dyer

IS IT TIME

Time to rise for labour at dawn,
Spreading her long golden legs throughout
The morning,
That she has decided to deliver to us,
A new-born child opposite of dusk.

Time to adopt to her new routine,
Of sunshine smiles and rain clouded frowns,
sharing these moods each day from her decades
far away,
Reaching but once the brilliance of noon
where she longs to stay.

Time to settle into a sedate solar state,
Of retrospective sunset thoughts ablaze within
the night,
With fleeting moments of warm caresses,
That she's beamed to all addresses.

Time no more her cycle complete,
She's secretly aged throughout her journey,
Of being a lonely, solitary, living flash,
Her momentary bygones - going nowhere fast.

Timeless she belongs among the stars,
Within an eternal light dimension,
Wandering, carefree unhurried she knows,
It is time for her glorious heavenly show!

V Miles

THE DISAPPEARING VALLEYS

Each time I travel through the valleys, I stare through the window of the bus,
I see mountains with broad gaps and landslides, the valleys are leaving us.
These gaps and cracks turn the mountain into giant snakes and ladders,
No ferns or bulrushes, all little creatures swept away, including the adders.
So many dead trees like grey skeletons scattered all around,
Some green trees are surviving, leaning just above the ground,
People driven from their homes for fear of being buried alive.
Some houses with cracked walls ready to take a dive,
The sight of these giant mountains crumbling away is so sad
The rumble of the landslides driving the inhabitants mad,
Many sheep still wander around the grey stone and dust,
The farm owner refusing to leave his home, in God he put his trust.
Our childhood days were spent on the mountains, we had many happy hours.
The smell of bluebells, the violets, so many pretty wild flowers.
The little streams of pure clear water, we drank to quench our thirst,
Then run down the mountain, wonder, who would reach the bottom first.
Man is the culprit man is helping to destroy the earth,
Cutting down the giant trees, draining the oil from the earth,
The blasting of the rocks to make new roads day after day,
The old coalmines with their long tunnels just falling away,
The continuous pounding of the mountain for the lime stone quarries.
Buildings shaking from the constant flow of heavy lorries.
The beauty of the valleys maybe lost forever, looking dull and grey
Just to make man a lot of money, man is taking the beauty away.

M L Webb

THE RELAY RACE

A streak of fear ran down my spine
While standing on the starting line.
The whistle blew
And off I flew
   Down to Andrew Mac
   Who grabbed the stick
   So mighty quick
   And off went he,
   So pleased to be
   In the lead
   And then . . .
   Lisa grabbed the stick from him
   And ran like Sebby Coe.
   Down the track
   No looking back
   Till Phil she saw
   And feared no more
   In this case
   Because Phil's ace
   And he went on
   To win the race.

Maurice Chambers

WHO AM I?

Look at me, Oh look at me.
Who do you see when you look at me?
Do you see a mother, do you see a wife?
Do you see someone with no other life?

Look at me, oh look at me.
Who do you see when you look at me?

Oh please, see me.

Irene E Rowlands

A RAY OF HOPE

Alternative medicine, is the one for me
It makes me feel very healthy.
A garlic pearl, a once a day
Helps keep the doctor at bay
Only natural ingredients are used
In every product the is produced.
Staying healthy is not a sin
So go on give Healthy
Alternatives a spin.

M Jones

ENEMY

As if it never existed,
It disappeared,
No trace, no feeling,
Nothing but silence,
No distant echo, no screams,
Silent movement,
Everything crowding,
A blank expression on its face,
Trapped in silence,
No longer nightly dreams,
Contaminated signs,
Surviving alone,
Dying in numbers,
For a moment it came,
Left a trail in the sky,
No one cared anymore,
Marooned in silence,
    The enemy had gone . . .

Ross I Standring

A TRIBUTE TO THE ANONYMOUS GRAVES

The sirens, the Blitz. The bombs, direct hits
The death of the innocent and the brave
The youngsters enlisted to fight for the twisted
Ended up in anonymous graves.

The kids not understanding played *war* on the landing
As the real war raged on from the skies
And on land and at sea was the fight to be free
Amidst bloodshed and tears and cries.

Though I wasn't there. No, not even born
My father was there, his Lancaster torn
And ripped from the sky and roared to the ground
Alive, but aflame in a field he was found.

And when he woke badly burned in his hospital bed
Lucky was he. His best mates were dead
And they say 'We won the war.' A falsehood. A lie
Nobody wins when so many die.

And a thought for those who have fought and have died
Lost their lives with passion and anger and pride
And each night I pray there'll be no more world war
Because by the end of the next there'd be nowt to fight for.

Gerard Phillips

STEPHEN

I love you more than life itself yet I cannot tell you why
But I'll carry that love inside of me, until the day I die.
Then when I meet my maker, my sins to be revealed,
my soul to go I know not where, my ashes in a field
Remember that I love you and that I always cared,
and one day we will meet again sometime, some place, somewhere.

F Kettle

REUNION

Grey and white
Yellow with age
Blackened with soot
Grainy photographs mirror silently
distant places . . . happier faced buttercups . . .
Time satisfied . . .
Time past.
Chipped orange vase holds wild flowers
Brittle and dusty.
Tattered lace curtain stutters a hello
flaps goodbye.
A leaf sputters through
open window.
The space between the weathered door
and worn road is blue.
A soft wind stirs up kinder
fragrances of - Welsh cakes baking
Freshly cut grass upon a larger
sea of green - the Past.
Lazy shadows drift over vale and hill
A spray of sun sneaks through
spot lighting mustard coloured field.
In a whisper shadows fade
Grey and white photographs
distant faces . . .
Unite in dreams.

John Thomas Jones

WALES

This land of independent folk
The home of spiritual song
A green and rainy countryside,
The place where I belong.

More beautiful than any scene
Captured on a canvas
The secret lies within the wind
Which carries hope to warm us.

Farmers toil upon their hills,
Souls at one with nature;
A language and a land apart
From all who try to change her.

For those who stay to savour Wales
With all her Celtic legends,
There is the price she strangely claims -
Acceptance of her customs.

This ancient land encompasses
Minds and hearts which know
The spirit in the breeze, the soul in the leaves,
And a pride which will never go.

Diane Antoniazzi

AGE OF WONDER

Have we travelled too far
In the age of the motor car
Contamination on winds, in tides
Synthetics and pesticides

Polluted rivers, acid rain
Will radiation leak again
How far should we progress
With natural balance under stress

A new language rules our lives
Evidence of how man strives
For micro-chips and laser beams
Atoms and researching genes

Advantages for the minority
While scientists hold the key
Can nature answer to the call
To re-dress the balance for us all

B E Eyre

WATCHING THE WORLD GO BY

I sit and watch the world go by,
it won't be very long.
I sit and watch the world go by,
and hum a little sing.

And as I sit and watch it,
here in the morning sun.
I polish up my bayonet,
my sword and knife and gun.

I went out to the battle,
and deeds I did aplenty.
Of enemy soldiers that I killed,
were more than five and twenty.

And when the war was over,
I made my way back home.
But everything had passed away,
all I'd ever known.

And now I sit and watch the world,
at the closing of the day.
Old soldiers they will never die,
they simply fade away.

Richard W Finlan

SO PRECIOUS

A tree is such a precious thing,
It stands so strong, its trunk is stout,
Its branches growing up and out,
As if to reach the clear blue sky.

Its beauty is quite breath taking,
Especially when its buds are breaking,
The lovely shapes that it is making,
The different shades of green,
Is a wonder to be seen.

To sit beneath a full grown tree,
And see the beauty of its leaves surround me,
It's then that I can really feel,
The wonder of nature that is all around me.

A tree can give us shelter from a storm,
And then in winter keep us warm,
We can feel its deep strength growing from within,
For a tree is really a living thing,
To feel the sheer joy that it can bring,
Oh, a tree is such a precious thing.

Terri Brant

THE TRAGEDY OF DUNBLANE

I hear your sorrow
I feel your pain
How will things for you ever be the same
For off to school they went that terrible day
An evil man came and took their lives away
All their parents have left are the memories
Of the children they have lost to keep them at ease.

Geraint Rhys Leach

TRAFFIC LIGHT KIDS

I have three daughters, all girls you see,
They are so beautiful and precious to me.
First there is Jade a beautiful green.
So caring and loving and full of beans.
Next came Amber a golden glow,
A mummy's girl she goes where I go,
the third is Ruby chubby and bright,
She tries everything till she gets it right.
Why all the jewels God forbids,
But I just call them my traffic light kids.
We started on green, paused on orange,
Yes just two we know we can manage.
But another night of passion in the
marital bed,
A third was soon born, we stopped on red.

S J Evans

LOVE IS ...

Love is the strongest feeling in the universe,
Love is what people feel for each other when they get married,
Love is peace keeping,
Love is when you care for somebody.

Love is a feeling that no-one can deny,
Love is the feeling that finds you a partner for life,
Love is bigger that big,
Love is the ultimate problem solver.

Love is what built the world,
Love is shown in many ways,
Love is what conquers all,
Love is *wonderful!*

Russell Charles Franklin

HE'S MINE

Sweet love of my life,
I'll tell you why,
Your sweet smile.
Is well worthwhile
Your green eyes,
Your dimpled chin,
You're really cute, when you
grin.
Sweet love of my life,
I see only you,
In a crowded room, Oh yes
it's true.
People laugh, people shout,
But you, you're quiet, when
You're out.
I like to see you, in that
space,
You're the one my love
The one I grace.
You dark haired wonder
With the smiling face.
I love you.

Elaine Marshall

HOLIDAY TIME

Corfu, Corfu, here I come
14 days in the beautiful sun.
Slip on grit, broken leg
First nine days Corfu hospital bed.

Daughter Jill travelling far
Sometimes bus but mostly taxi car.
No sandy beaches no playing in the sun
Just wait for my daughter Jill to come

Bring some food for me to eat
The big tomato is really a treat.
July it all started I still limp about
One wrong move and I give a shout.

Not for much longer I really do hope
Then we will sit back and think it's all been a joke.

June Christensen

MY GRANDDAUGHTER

When my granddaughter and I sat down to tea,
She said 'What about the children not so lucky as me,
Some children live in a faraway land
Have no bed to sleep on, only the sand.
I have a mammy and daddy too.
Those children have no-one, and nothing to do.
They don't even have proper food to eat,
For them a piece of bread is a treat.
Chocolate and ice-cream they know nothing about,
Some of them don't even have the strength to shout.
Malnutrition, infection, sores, runny eyes,
When we see their pictures we want to cry.
So before you go to sleep tonight
Please think on these children in their sorry plight,
Ask our father up above
To try to send them some of our love,
For we believe thoughts are a living thing,
And one day to these children, hope we may bring.

M Y Briggs

THE BULLY

The pain that lingers in your head,
   The nightmares that you have in bed,
And all the things the bully said,
   Will never leave your mind

The tears rolling down your cheek,
   The teasing faced, week after week,
The help of which you cannot seek,
   Stay imbedded in your mind.

The things they break, not just your heart,
   Your confidence, even a part,
Of you which cannot be replaced,
   Until you speak your mind.

There is one thing you have to learn,
   Before your heart cannot burn,
With pain and fury your heart will turn,
   Until you speak and cry.

The pain of hitting, does not apply,
   When your best friend says goodbye,
Just because someone told a lie,
   And they cannot give a reason why.

The memories, all good and bad,
   When you think, it makes you sad,
Of all the things you could have had,
   Sometimes makes you raging mad.

But all these things have come true,
   Mostly to me, maybe to you,
So think of me, when you are sad,
   Of the friends you have, and be glad.

Catherine Page

FLAMES

As the glowing flames flickered
Reflected in her eyes
Her thought s deep in the past
Remembering goodbyes.

The one she loved so deeply
Had hurt her oh so bad
She'd thought that he would never leave
And never make her sad.

But late that autumn day
She'd awoke to see him there
With an open half-filled suitcase
Upon the bedroom chair.

He'd said that he was sorry
But he just had to leave
For he had found another love
To stay would just cause grief

He'd looked at her, then said goodbye
Her eyes had filled with tears
Don't go my love, she'd softly said
Please stay with me, stay here

But words had not meant anything
And he'd turned and closed the door
Now her life was an empty shell
And he was there no more

Just flames of fire to warm her
Like the flames of love once true
If only he'd come back to her
To change the flames so blue.

G Jones

BILL

With baited breath Bill said to me,
Help me Jack for I cannot see,
The bullet lodged in his head
His brain shot like molten lead.
As I knelt down by his side,
His glazed eyes opened wide,
My heart was heavy for my *friend*
But I knew his head, it could not mend.
'Please Jack end my misery
And from this pain I will be free.
Pull the trigger Jack, end my life
And take a message to my wife
Tell her that I didn't linger on,
That I carried her love through the Somme.'
I shot him, tears were flowing free
He would have done the same for me.
I closed his eyes and kissed his hand
He was gone from the carnage of this land.
Cease-fire came, the land was still,
Thousands died that day with Bill.
The memory haunts me, as I grow old
Just the thought, makes me go cold.
To me, like Bill there'll be no others
For Bill and me, we were brothers.

Sylvia Currey

AFTERMATH

She trudges along the promenade,
Weighed down with bags and packs,
Holiday makers stare and say
'Why does she carry those old sacks?'
Her clothes are clean; her face aglow
From the open air and sun.
Why does she carry all those bags?
Is her journey never done?
Folks say she sleeps in open air
Could one believe this so?
And then I met a passer by
Who said 'Oh yes, it's true.
The woman has a darkened life
That none of us could know.
Once- she'd had a home
All sparkling, bright, and clean
She'd dust and polish each new day
'Till roof to floor would gleam.
One night - Time of the war you know
There was a ghastly raid
Her house fell down around her
And in it she was laid.
She did not die and life went on,
Though 'twas never quite the same
Her fear of bricks and stone and walls
She never overcame.'
And so she lives free as the air,
Sun, moon and stars her friends
Her solace is the open road
Her journeying never ends.

Doreen Davies-Paton

INSPIRATIONS

I see my inspirations,
And I read them through.
I hear my inspirations,
And I hope that you will too.
I feel my inspirations,
And my tongue does taste a few.
I search for my inspirations,
And I find them all around.
I gather my inspirations,
And they wait, oh so patiently, to be found.
I reach for my inspirations,
And I grab them when I can.
I judge my inspirations,
And justice helps me plan.
I time my inspirations,
And hope the seconds will not count.
I crave my inspirations,
And will one day let them out.
I capture my inspirations,
And imprison them with glee.
For all my inspirations,
Will one day be free.

Y King

AN EAGLE

I soar above the rock and crags
   of mountains far below.
The white foam water of the stream
   crashes down the rifts
'til spent, it breaths a sigh
   and spreads exhausted, in a fan
     far out to sea.

Above all this I fly the calm
   and fresh clear skies
and gaze in awed serenity
   at the world beneath me
in all its troubled ways
   and wish to stay untouched;
I am an eagle.

John Gilchrist

CRUMLIN VIADUCT

Across the tracks, the train came,
Linking the two valleys, things would never be the same.
The viaduct was built for all to see,
to linger on, in our memory.

In 1853 it all began,
When Mr Thomas William Kennard, had a wonderful plan.
The work was complete in 1855,
the job that made us feel alive.

In June 1857 the day finally came,
the day when Crumlin, would never be the same.
The first train to cross this famous viaduct,
to bring the valley prospects and a bit of luck.

The most joyous of occasions, for us all to see,
hoping this would remain and forever be.
But in 1964 the sad day did arise,
the last train to cross her,
We could not believe our eyes.
The sadness we felt, was hard to express,
then in 1965, she was put to rest.

Helen Rees-Smith

SAVED

Since I was a child,
I've always despised men;
My father left
Just after my sixth birthday.
I never dreamed I'd find happiness,
So I found warmth in
One night stands.
Once one night turned into a year
And two months.
We were fine at first -
I trusted you,
You let me be
My own person,
Never argued when I wanted time
To myself,
To find myself.
But soon you grew tired
And craved attention
I couldn't give you.
You took too much space,
My friends stopped calling round.
So one night I took a pillow
And placed it over your face.
You never struggled
Or made a sound.
I felt relieved;
I'd saved my daughter
From a world full of men.

Samantha Cowlin

UNTITLED

A tribute to Dunblane
A prayer to help the pain
A day in our lives we'll never forget
When sixteen children were slain

There are no words to explain
The tragic events at Dunblane
Sweet little children took safely to school
Whose lives were took by a madman a fool

They say there's a God somewhere up there
If that's the case he's so unfair
He's left these families broken hearted
In such the way that they were parted

They'd gone to school to read and write
But soon their day was turned to night
Darkness fell the world left crying
As teachers, children lay there dying

A minutes silence we'll all give
A beautiful rose garden for them to live
One consolation they'll have each other
But heartache and tears for every mother

As I write this we all feel the same
Our hearts go out to the village of
        Dunblane.

Christine Lyons

NAN

We may not see your charming face,
or see your cheering smile.
But when I think of all the times,
when I was just a child.
You always were the busy one,
doing the household chores ;-
cooking, cleaning, sewing - who
could have asked for anything more?
You always were the strongest one,
Keeping heart and soul adhered.
A family girl, with loving arms, and
radiating tenderness, exuding endless charm.
You lived your life of hardship, with
an optimism unknown - to us, you
left behind a sorrow and grief so bold.
You always had an answer, over the
questions we pined.
Your wit and logic surround us, and
hope that your presence will always
be felt.
For no-one can replace you, or even
come as close, to provide the care,
and attention, that you gave us
for so long.
Goodnight, God bless, we love you,
in our hearts we always will!

Lyn Maureen Jones

NIGHTMARE

Words in my head,
Must get them out,
Can't sleep
Tried counting sheep,
Higgledy piggledy,
Jumping about,
Must sort them out
Get them down
Make them rhyme,
All these words
In my head.

M E O'Brien

FROSTY FLAKES

The snow is soft as wool, as silver flakes
fall down
The stars are twinkling like silver rings that
hang up in the sky
The crunchy leaves are being cracked by cold
feet
Christmas lights are shining like candles that
make the darkness bright
The icy ponds shine like the moon light
Most of the children are snuggled up in bed
Like animals asleep now
Faces at the window looking at the frosty
snow fall down.

Rhys Oliver Hodge

THE LESSON

What loss is mine, I can only but gain
betrayed by one whose words are not true,
What loss is mine, when danger approaches
to see him cower like a pet at his master's feet
but the feet are not those of his master, she is not there,
they are but the feet of his master's friend
whose friendship he fears to lose, and mine he fears to keep.

Kay S Dunn

CASTLES

As I sit building castles in the sand
My heart is in a far off wonderland,
Of fairy tales I heard in nursery rhyme,
And as my lovely castle grows
I wander through the mists of time.

There is a lovely place I'll surely know
Called *Once-upon-a-time-long-long-ago*
I'll build a castle there with shining towers,
With forests wild, and gleaming swans
And everywhere most wondrous flowers.
I'll find the purest gold, and ivory.
(For I will build my castle halls romantically)
And when my princess comes (a maid most fair)
She'll find her knight in shining armour there,

And as I build this castle in the sand
My heart is in that far off wonderland,
But then comes in, relentlessly, the tide -
And so - my lovely castle goes,
And fades into the mists of time.

Paula Favorido

THAT OTHER WORLD

White haired, a stooped back and with a stick prodding uncertainly as he returns to his cell . . . It is his home and he is worried sick for his release day is almost here and he has nowhere to go. What friends he has are here on the landing with him and they have the same fear. Their freedom will be the cold street and shop doorways with hand outs from the Sally Ann soup wagon if they are lucky.

Shaven headed with a scowl on his face and hate filled eyes as he waits for mail-call . . . Has she sent any cash this time? He needs a new Walkman, the old one is in pieces after being thrown at the cell wall in a fit of childish rage. It was this rage that got him sentenced but he learned nothing from the experience . . . Why did that old woman kick up such a fuss?

Next door to the old man lives the wing academic who views the rest of his fellow inmates with a thinly veiled contempt. . . He reads books by Jung and Nietzche and claims to understand them but for some reason he cannot look a woman in the eye . . .

Then there is the old lag who knows more about prisons than most of the staff ever will . . .To him, being locked away is a hazard of his job. He knows the rules and can live happily with them for the length of his sentence. His wife and kiddies visit often and it is obvious that his eldest lad wants to follow in his dad's footsteps.

And me? I'm a warder, a screw . . . too stupid or too idle to do a proper job but everyday I listen to excuses and reasons why so and so is here. They forget that I know . . .I've read the records but I bite my tongue and let the self delusions continue. . .

D Lapham

VILLAGE LIFE

I wandered lonely as a sheep
That roams on high o'er vales and hills
Then all of us formed a crowd
And ate up all your daffodils.
You can spend lots of dosh, securing your gate
But to ruin your garden we cannot wait
Tens of us you will see at a glance
We'll make you scream shout and dance.
By your fence beneath your bush
If you've got flowers we'll push and push
But we'll find a way in just wait and see
Then munch upon your garden with glee.

Joanne Griffiths & Thomas Griffiths

THE BOMB

What is blue, Mother?
Blue was the sky, child.
What is green, Mother?
Green was the grass and trees, child.
What are trees, Mother?
Trees were breath and life, child.
Where are they now, Mother?
Gone, child, gone forever.

What is love, Mother?
Love is my lullaby for you, child;
Hush now and sleep,
Sleep on forever.
Do not wake to this evil, child,
This evil cloud of death.

Claire M Bellamy

STOLEN MOMENTS

Further than the horizon
exquisite beauty lays.
You feel the stimulating
Freshness of the ocean's water,
as waves crash over the rocks.
Your heart touching faraway lands,
as the warmth of the sun
caress the contours of your skin.
There are vibrant wild flowers
pushing up from the soil.
From the depths of the earth's garden,
you smell the exotic fragrances
blowing in the breeze.
Mouth watering fruit,
hanging plentiful from the trees.
Birds, calling from above.
A marvellous moment of pleasure,
a true sense of well being.
Snatched away from reality.

Anne Valeria Davies

FORGOTTEN DREAMS?

When the twilight sets on our precious lives,
Will you still remember me?
When your life is an empty shell,
Will you still remember me?
When you struggle weary to your bed,
Will you remember our youth and happiness?
When you sit by the fire in your chair,
Will you remember the fun that we shared?
When you look at the jaded photographs,
Will you remember the dreams we had?

Venetia Hogben

RACISM

Does it matter what colour we are?
Whether we're as white as snow or as black as tar,
We're all the same, deep down inside,
So why do people have to hide?

Ignorance surely reigns supreme,
Or is it intentional - it sometimes seems,
I'm just like you if you stop and think,
I too have to eat and also to drink.

I also have emotions, feelings and pride,
I'm exactly the same as you inside,
It's only my skin that's different, you see,
Out ancestors fought for us all to be free.

So just stop and think when you show your hate,
Different colours doesn't mean second rate,
My heart beats the same as yours, you see,
Just look beyond the colour and there you'll find me.

Sian Matthews

BAD TIMES

A place where only I can go.
Not a real world that you would know.
It's deep and low there is no light.
My spirit dies without a fight.

A loved one's voice is all it takes.
Such real tears they are not fake.
The world goes on but I do not.
Do they know, will I be forgot.
The future sits so far away.

Another time maybe another day.
Night has taught all it can teach.
Morning seems so hard to reach.

The way is clear that I must be.
A light is there for me to see.
With my love's help I will fight.
To find the day and leave the night.

Andrew Byard

MY PERSONAL STORM

A sniggering silence, cunningly hides
Behind a long and tiresome day
I feel and sense the smell of wrath
Like jaws of fire devouring its prey

The hunger, the panic the clutching of straws
The anchor of life is shaken
Loosening its hold, breaking away,
Alone and cruelly forsaken.

Anger thrust upon innocent eyes
Distorted images strong
Voices screaming, shouting, weeping
The agony lingers on

Demands beyond my control
The lightning, the thunder the pain
The downpour that follows will drown,
The rage, the hurt and the shame.

In the midst of this frightening song
A lull in the tempest prevails
The sea will be calm and at ease
And silence will know it has failed.

Linda Roberts

I THINK IT'S TIME

I think it's time,
I tried to live my own life,
Not just through another's eyes.

Every second that passes, never to be returned,
Is a wasted opportunity spurned.
I'm here for a reason,
We all are I'm sure,
But most of the time I feel like a mistake, a blip, a nothing man.

Sometimes I don't want to go to sleep,
It's a waste of precious time.
But I never do anything when I'm awake.
My grip is weak and the days well oiled,
Tomorrow might just be too late.

I'm not old in years,
But inside I never feel young.
The fire has died down,
I can't find the spark.

I think,
No, I know it's time,
I try to live my own life.
Here goes.

V Topp

TIME SHARE

There he stands in the checkout queue,
Old and slow and in front of you
Who have so many chores.
He must be thick, he just ignores
The sighs and drumming finger tips.
A smile plays round his thin blue lips
As he chats to the checkout operator.

He's storing her words to remember later
When he's back and terribly alone
In the shell of the place he once called home.
A good girl that to understand
That old folk often need a hand
In a world that moves much too fast
For those whose minds reach back to the past.

Gillian Avis

SHADOWS

A frightened mother and her child scurry through the sinister streets,
Looking wearily this way and that for signs
Of any unusual activity.
It's been tranquil, too tranquil, and it shows in their faces.
The shadows of another world, another life are there portrayed.
A darkness borne of horror which has long been here, a sense of
Expectation of something not wanted anymore.

A bomb blast, the crack of gunfire, the screaming
Sounds of innocent people being slaughtered.
And you stand there and have the audacity to call it a peace process?
Cease-fire, peace-fire, to us it doesn't mean a thing.
From Londonderry in the north to Omagh in the west
A fear grips the people like a shadow hanging on for dear life.
We can't forget and we remember
Those days, months and years of trepidation and insecurity.
Enniskillen and Armagh to you are just memories;
Our soldiers, *our* sons and *our* lovers fought
To prove a point long forgotten in this bloody conflict.

We wait and we wonder, but we know that they are there
Just waiting in the corners - and the shadows.
A quarter of a century have now passed with ever-growing cemeteries and
The differences between us are still clearly visible.
Doesn't over three thousand wasted lives mean anything to you?

Barry Townsend

THIS THAT I DON'T UNDERSTAND

My eyes, heavy close,
Fearful anticipation evokes,
The darkness comes forth,
Concealing its cold truths and secrets,
Her face basked within its history,
A past to which I neither feature nor belong,
A pain that eats, eroding the present,
I can feel this tangible emotional slashing,
Strong as I am, there's something here that blinds me,
This tidal flood of realisation consumes,
My world, so small, tightens and constricts,
I suffocate within my thoughts,
This pain that I don't understand, won't be denied,
My dreams envelope, I struggle through this waking sleep,
My senses overload, my head says walk, my heart says fight,
But I lack the tools, my love, too weak,
I feel defeated before I've begun,
So many objections, so many obstructions,
I am seemingly insufficient,
I don't fit, don't belong, don't deserve,
I am a burden, a waste, the proverbial milestone,
I am bombarded by opinions, all share a common ground,
I'm so lucky, she's so great, so perfect, so much,
Well I am, so lucky and I don't deserve,
Next week, next month, next year,
This fact will dawn,
She will agree,
And I won't mend.

M S Drabble

OUR NURSES

What do you see you ask, what do you see?
Yes, we are thinking when looking at thee
We may seem to be hard when we hurry and fuss
But there are too many of you, and too few of us
We would like far more time, to sit by you and talk
To bathe you - to feed you, to teach you to walk
To hear of your life, the things that you've done
Your childhood, your husband, your daughter, your son.
But time is against us, there's too much to do
Patients are many, and nurses too few
We grieve when we see you so sad and alone
With nobody near you, no friend of your own
We feel all your pain, and know of your fear
That nobody cares now, that your end is near
But nurses are people, with feelings as well
And when we are together, you often hear tell
Of the dear old granny in the very end bed, and the lovely
Old man, and the stories he has said.
We speak of the compassion, and love, and feel sad
When we think of your lives, and the joy that you have had,
When the time has arrived for you to depart
You leave us behind, with an ache in our heart
When you sleep the long sleep, no more worry or care
There are other patients awaiting, and we must be there
So please, understand when we hurry and fuss
There are too many of you, and too few of us. . .

W James

THE SEA

The sea is rough
The sea is tough
The sea is furious
The sea is monstrous
The sea is angry
The sea is cruel
The sea is lively
The sea is wicked
The sea is unkind
The sea is creepy
but I still like the sea.

James Channing

THE WALES I KNOW

Wales, Wales
It's a magical place
With leeks and daffodils
At its grace,
Rugby men are running round
Passing and falling to the ground

Wales is a place with all the mines
Ironworks, industries and railway lines,
Hillsides, farming, running streams
It's a beautiful place for all it seems

Wales is a land for singing a song
The male voice choirs go hand in hand,
Land of my fathers, we'll share a beer
Because this great country has no fear,
We'll serve this country from day to day
Hoping and loving it all the way!

Marc A C Redman

PICASSO'S PIGEONS

They came with a buoyancy
To claim your hand in silent hours
In deft movements, the rustling of chalk,
With the gentle clarity of flowers,
They accompanied you in your darkest day,
A polystyrene freight of the soul,
Offering morse code, fragmented talk
Of fragile woodwind call.

You placed them in spirit cages
Remedy, to your matador rages,
Virginal doves ensnared in your play,
Sometimes poised on a balcony,
Or flying over the ochre hide of Spain,
Innocently against horizon's red pain
White stars over the rocky terrain,
Ice-fire of the continental bay
Stars knocked from their perch,
Taken in your colossal stony clutch.

Jacqueline Jones

LIFE SAVER

Swim, swim the ocean wide
ducking and diving
you dare not sleep
The ocean is so far and wide
strength is on your side
even though you cannot trust it
and yes you must respect
the ocean is so far and wide
Hence ne're we do forget!

C Fisher

STOLEN LULLABY

Warm winds softly fall
Breathing o'er hills and meadows
Looking for the rippling river
To make an unexpectant call.
Blackbird sing in weeping willow tree
Blend with voice of wind and river
Awake'ing a new found melody.
Light winds dance to birth of spring
They circle ripples in mother river
Like a dove that spreads it wings.
Each ripple in river reflect a child
All smile to new found music
Enchant the near by rose growing wild.
Song bird watch in silence
From weeping willow tree
As strong wings falls o'er river
To collect the chosen melody.
Warm winds in peace to bring
Gather young ripples from river
Carry back to heaven
Under her snow white wings.
Music from heaven
Send to earth a new lullaby
To comfort all weeping mothers
Until to meet again
In the sweet bye and bye.

Phyllis Blue

POST MODERNIST POET IN WALES MAPS

Poets must keep true,
While the Welsh redraw maps.
In Talgarth,
Poor old ladies,
Gym skirt girls, boys with ties,
For all the heaps of books,
They did not know
The place of vision.

Million encounters,
The television soaps,
Bypass, Horse Treck. A Glider Field,
Spar shop, Jobs,
EU and Councillors' Fees,
All seem to know.

No sign up lane
To the monastery
At Capel y Fin,
Worse in Llanbrynmaier,
For the Hen Capel,
'You are the very first to ask.'

Few know of Samuel Roberts,
Howell Harris or Pantycelyn.
Nation, once awake,
Rubbed off the map of Wales.

Paul Faulkner

UNTITLED

Went to town to do some shopping
Saw the other shoppers stopping
Thought to myself, what can it be
Then I saw the team from the BBC

Swarms of people all excited
Wondered if I'd get invited
To talk to That's Life handsome Glyn
But he didn't notice me

As I stood there in the crowd
My heart it was a thumping loud
Oh Glyn it cried, please look my way,
Make mine a happy St David's Day

But sad to say was not to be
There seemed no opportunity
I stood and thought what might have been
If he had looked, and I'd been seen

Now every time when I'm in town
I still see Glyn walk up and down
With mike in hand, a smile on his face
For me now Newport's a That's Life place.

Rae Jones

THE SEA EMPRESS

Ship on the rocks, what a disaster
Oh she needs help where is her master.
Spewing black oil out of its tanks.
Look out! look out! she's on the mud banks.

Little tug boats pull with all of their might
She won't refloat, she'll be there until night,
Driving rain, and the wind blows a gale.
They try once again but endeavour to fail.

Waves crashing into her and over her hull,
She's stuck fast, so they'll wait for a lull,
Oil slicks spread out over the sea.
Capturing sea birds that want to be free.

They try once again and with luck on their side,
She's pulled to safety on the next tide.
It could have been avoided if she hadn't been forsaken,
Money doesn't matter, time should have been taken.

Lynda Byard

CHRISTMAS LAMENT

'Tis the night before Christmas.
And I'm feeling depressed.
The veggies are clogging the sink!
The turkey's not cooking
The pudding's gone off!
And no-one will give me a drink!

I've not wrapped the presents.
I've forgotten the port
And everyone's as evil as sin
Won't somebody save me from Yule tide fun?
I've decided I never can win

So roll on the new year
Goodbye to all this.
Let Christmas be flushed down the pan
    I'm sick as a parrot!
    I'm poor as a tramp!
I'm afraid that it's all hit the fan
    Boom! Boom!

Maureen Nixon

POSTCARDS FROM BEVVY

These are a few of the places I have been
Done many things, many a thing seen
Travelled the world on different cruise ships
Working so hard, getting paid in good tips
Departed London, Gatwick, Heathrow
Bound for America, Caribbean,Mexico
Arrived In Miami, Tampa, Fort Lauderdale
These are home ports, collected our mail
Went to Cozumel, Jamaica, Barbados, Key West
Alaska, Vancouver, LA, Acapulco is best
California I've been there
Felt the wind blow through my hair
East coast, west coast, Panama Canal
Places to go, shop in the mall
Sun shining hot, Catching a tan
Nowhere to run, but Grand Cayman
Drinking cocktails all day by the sea
Pina Colada, Long Island ice tea
Visited places San Juan and St Croix
Sailed the Pacific and Atlantic ocean, ship ahoy
Swam with the dolphins and scuba dive
Glad to be happy and alive
Met a lot of 'very good' friends
Been to paradise, but it all comes to an end.

Beverley Elliott

AN ENGLISHMAN ABROAD (IN WALES)

The English and Welsh are nothing alike,
Their countries are parted by king Offa's dyke,
So why are the English attracted to Wales?
For in spite of our climate they visit our vales.
Well! They're on foreign land without crossing the sea,
And feel really abroad when they're in Anglesy.
They don't need a passport to visit our land,
And no customs officials to check contraband.
No travellers cheques or changing of money,
And during high season it might even be sunny;
When the Welsh get together and chat in a throng,
They are very aware that they do not belong;
If they don't know the language they don't stand a chance,
They feel more abroad than if they were in France;
And our Welsh hospitality is really innate,
There's tea, bara brith and Welsh cakes on a plate;
Nor are we alike in ways or in features,
English and Welsh are such different creatures;
The resorts in the north they haven't despised,
For Prestatyn and Rhyl have become Anglisised;
And they visit the Arms Park of rugby renown,
Where Welsh voices are raised to win triple crown.
For to sing in tune and harmony is natural to Celt,
To diminish English hopes is surely their intent;
Yet they visit our country, of legend and myth,
Where we proudly display a Cymru -Am-Byth,
For what the Welsh have always preserved as a nation,
Is hospitality, perhaps because of their isolation;
And I'm sure any Englishman would be bound to agree,
When in Wales he's abroad without crossing the sea.

June Lane

ALWAYS THE TREES (IN CWM DYLI)

I keep coming back to the trees
Time after time; each visit
Draws me to their precarious plight,
To their undeciphered and aged wisdom.

How precarious, can be measured
By their scarcity; their rarity;
Their age, even their infirmity
In this unforgiving landscape.

The few survivors of man's quest for fuel
And sheep's jaw, perch almost unattainable.
Their offspring succumb
To the normal fate of their kind.

Today, in windswept flurries of snow,
I visited them all - twenty seven
At last count. I felt their desire
To bear children in this changing place.

Derek Mayes

A GYPSY REQUEST

Would you care to walk with me?
Will you tread the way?
Will you watch the evening fall
And grace the dawn of day?

Would you share my fireside
As I would share my life with you,
Aye, share the good and bad with me
And make my dreams come true.

And I will share those dreams right well
With a true and honest heart,
And keep my love within my dreams
Until we're forced to part.

And even when the parting comes
Twill only seem a day
And then we'll walk the moon and stars
Till time has passed away.

Peter Kuck

STEEL STRIKE

They came and they raped all the valleys
They ground all us Welsh in the dust
They treated and worked us like cattle
Begrudgingly threw us a crust.

These are the words passed down by our Grandfathers
Who lived through those terrible times
And we their Grandsons can tell you
Of being exploited, despised and defiled.

We remember the soul destroying thirties
When it was working on short time or dole
When the means-test man called on a Tuesday
To make sure we paid what we owed.

If one week we missed a small payment
To buy a new shirt or some shoes
The next time we went for our money
That amount from our dole we did lose.

So we gave full support of BI SAKTA
Made it strong so that its voice could be heard
Helped turn the wheel right around in full circle
So that the strength of the worker is feared.

Ralph May

UNTITLED

Love could make poets of us all,
if only we would let it.
But if we did, what would befall
all those who are indebted,
for inspiration to love's call,
so they can write, to please us all,
of passions pure and otherwise,
soft words, flowers, clear blue skies?

Would they then resort to writing about sensible things
in order to keep their bank balances in the black?

Brian Cox

HOPE

Never give up hope
Until you know the score
Life around you every day
Will seem so far at war
Hold on to your guns don't give up yet
Hope will bring them home
Safely I bet
Without hope what have you got
I'll tell you this it's not a lot
Hope to me is a key word
For loved ones who are at war
In Bosnia
Or anywhere they were fighting for peace
before
Before this world nearly came to an end
Remember this message comes from a
friend.

Rhian W Roberts

THE FLIGHT OF THE CRYSTAL GYPSY

Hey sweet Malandra,
The highway signs all point to you,
The sandman sleeps in vain,
Reminds me of the time visions came true.

And left alone the darkness falls,
And night time blankets all my hopeless dreams,
Magicians' wands and casting spells,
Paint clouded times that are never what they seem.

The prophecy of love,
Hangs its head so silently to you,
The distant sky that beckons life,
Holds gauntlet to the times that you once knew.

And silken sands you tread upon,
Burn my thoughts that you'll return to me,
The ragman plays hit mandolin along the coast,
And if you soul search you'll find your better off than most.

Hey sweet Malandra,
The knave turns to the king of hearts for you,
A gift of light that shines to earth,
That dance on hearts like others seldom do.

And the El Dorados in your dreams,
Are closer now than they have ever been,
The faceless people that claim were friends,
Seem distant now, a twisted bitter end.

Mick Maddiver

SUMMER

Winter has gone and springtime too
Summer is here and the sky so blue
Brightness everywhere and flowers arrayed
As if for inspection in a grand parade
There are roses, lilac, of blue and white
Wallflowers and pansies for our delight
Border plants and full blossomed trees
And among the flowers, the drone of the bees
Buttercups and daises in a field of green
And knee length grass where no one has been
Fern on the mountain where heather grows wild
Sheep graze in the meadows meek and mild
Horses lay in the heat of the sun
While their foals jump free enjoying the fun
Hedgerow full of surprising things
The beauty that only summer brings.

M Hodges

THE THINKER

They look, they stare, they touch and feel,
That create in their minds, what thought, what deed?
Of envy, I have time to think and ponder,
Of life's mysteries, and majestic wonder.
Why, wherefore, whatever, what with,
Shall I live and love, and be fulfilled
Knowledge, deep, in recess of mind, hidden
To find, and forage, and store when bidden.
Faith, sure and pure, seep in every pore
Will shake you to your very core
I have the answer, to all your mistakes
Come, my brother, open your eyes, and he awakes.

Rhoda Lewis

THE EBONY TREE

The Ebony Tree prayed for the moon, salvation
And restoration.
Twisting and curling, moving and grinding
Against the sweet silhouette of the sun.
Dancing to the sour melody of the night,
Hauntingly beautiful in its effect.
It licks the rain and spits out its tune,
Caresses the night air to make it warm.
This is the essence of the Ebony Tree.

The Ebony Tree waved to me, but I lack response,
Shimmering and glimmering, unsteady against the air.
Rippling and giggling it came towards me.
My dreams escape, but I do not.
My soul escapes, but I do not.
This is the essence of the Ebony Tree.

Jane Hunt

HOMELESS

How can we let these people live on the streets,
Like wandering leaves that brush past our feet,
Can we not help them you and I,
To make their lives easier under our sky,
Is it not time that houses were built,
For our young and our old who are cold and need heat,
Can we without guilt,
Leave them to others and just pass them by,
If we all took that attitude half the world would die,
We all need to campaign to make our views clear,
That we do not want this epidemic taking root here,
Remember on cold nights when winter's upon us,
While we are sleeping warm and dry in our beds,
That people are out there dying, frozen, underfed.

Katie Williams

KITCHEN MAGIC

If a dish was the moon,
And salt grains were the stars,
A spaceship could be a fork,
Travelling from Mercury to Mars.

The chair is an oil well,
And sugar the sound,
What of the fish smell,
That pollutes the land.

Saucers would be contact lenses,
Talcum powder the clouds,
The tin opener a Sergeant Major,
Who enjoys shouting loud.

Cereal boxes are prisons,
And knives the guards,
Flour must be cement,
That sets nice and hard.

If the cooker was a furnace,
Biscuits might be the coal,
Drinking straws are the footballer,
Who's just scored an own goal,

Spoons could be a graveyard,
Veg peelings a hill,
Spaghetti must be a thin man,
Complaining about his gas bill.

B Holland

SIMON'S SOLILOQUY

Simon is leaving, now that is a shame.
When things go wrong, who are we to blame?
When tension is high and tempers are fraught,
It's unfair to keep saying 'It's Peter's fault'.

The search is on for a new whipping boy
We urgently need someone new to employ.
Where do you get one that's so well trained.
Easy to wind up when we've moaned and complained?

His benevolence and humour we will dearly miss,
But not his sore head when he's been on the 'pop'?
In my consideration, when we've so much to do,
It's a terrible thing for him to put us all through.

We've really enjoyed mucking up his staff rota.
And had a good laugh when he's smacked up his motor.
Do you think we will now get some decent *'Pub grub'*
Will our wages be right, no more need for a sub.

We need an incentive to be nasty and rude
To deal with the customer that's throwing a mood.
His devotion to duty we can never attain,
Will work become dull, routine and mundane?

Off he goes on his way to earn lots of bread,
Not a thought for us all, does he have in his head.
For once I would like to have the last word
And tell him some home truths that I have heard.

People you've worked with are not what they seem,
For some strange reason you're held in high esteem.
They love you and wish you God speed in your quest
The final word being, 'He's one of the best'.

Carole Weeks

BIRD IN JULY

The sun ashines.
The roses bloom.
A garden's joy
And joy's perfume.

I hear in tune
A bird in song.
Do not tell me
That she is wrong.

For she is right.
Her sound, my sight.
A jewelled means
Of hope's delight.

Bird is happy.
And so am I.
May long her song
Embrace the sky.

May her glory,
Though small she be,
Accompany those
Who walk unfree.

Hywel Davies

DREAMS

What are these things that play in my sleepy mind?
That leave my outer self behind
That create a collision of my thoughts
And imagery of all sorts.

A contrast between fantasy and reality
Visions that only I can see
Making things happen to me and you
Creating yet another Dé jà vu.

The choice of what type, is not up to me
Romance, horror, real life or mystery
I wish I could choose; it's just not fair
When I end up with horror, and another nightmare.

They try to distract me when I'm awake
And assume my thoughts are theirs to take
These things that lead my mind astray
Call themselves dreams, people say.

Louise Ghosh

MIX-UP AT COMPUTER DATING AGENCY

The ad was in the Sunday Times, and quite eye-catching and in rhymes,
You'd pay by access, cheque was fine in currency of every clime.
If you are looking for a mate and think you've left it just too late,
Now don't just leave it up to fate, ring 'Perfect Partners' for a date.

Now poor judge Henry's feeling blue, he's just retired with nought to do;
He sees the Ad, the number too and rings, four twenty, six five two.
And sultry Debbie takes the call and says no problem, not at all
We've old and young and short and tall, we'll guarantee you to enthral.

We've got the best technology in this computer agency,
Complete the form and pay the fee and you'll be thrilled just wait and see,
Great, said Henry, I wont delay, I'll fill the form in right away,
Enclose a cheque your fee to pay and post it off this very day.

My, my he thought, that's all it takes though with excitement he now shakes.
And so it should barring mistakes which sultry Debbie often makes.
And so she sent him Didi Hari, who wore a yashmak and a sari,
Belly-danced from Rome to Pari with a snake she charmed, called Clary.

They made a date outside the Zoo and Clary had to be there too,
But three's a crowd that's very true, so Clary moved to pastures new.
Now Didi and judge Henry wed, her eastern smile just knocked him dead,
While Clary's found a home, it's said, in David Attenborough's shed.

Vivienne Bainton

THE GREATEST STORY IN THE WORLD

The world's greatest story will never be told
It seems, by you or I.
For you hold the secret away inside
In the darkness never to be seen,
At play in a field hidden deep down within
In a vault under lock and key.

The world's greatest story will never be told
It seems, by you or I,
And though my own memories are scars that I bear
On the outside for all to see,
They still go unnoticed to the sharpest of eyes;
Paled by time and the ache of deceit.

The world's greatest story will never be told
It seems, by you or I.
But perhaps one day in the riddles of time
When all has been laid down to rest,
Then release has collected our souls from this plain
And our carriage to life disconnects. . .
Someone will come to blow away the dust
From the memories I left from my fall,
And shed a few tears on the pages they read
From the greatest love story of all.

Gareth Jonn Owens

THE SILVER MOON

The silver moon in
The night makes
My love for you
Go wild.

The shining stars,
Softly gleam, but,
Then I think it is
Only a dream.

Michelle Beth Thomas

VISIONS OF THE NILE

Sounds of the adhan
Moan into the dusking air,
Spires of smoke and drifting smells of wood.
A tiny fishing boat juggles with the wake,
Man beating the waters to secure his catch.
Date Palms dust the fertile scape,
Banana clusters challenge the sugar and the wheat.
Sounds of laughter; images of waving, calling, whistling, never crying.
Luminous children and dowdy men.
Outlines of minarets scraping the ruddy sky,
A battered felucca sail; a low roofed muddied house.
Igret birds, swallows and kingfishers swooping low,
Distanced mountains - graves of years gone by.

Exhaustingly surreal and breathtakingly timeless:
This is the Nile.

Mari-Clare Pearman

STILL

The blind boy sees everything we told him to
But how could anybody be so cruel
Destroyed the feelings
Of another one who felt so plain
Ideas dreamed and wrote
Settles in his mind again
With steep success
His whole world was torn apart
They quickly came
So quickly that they should depart
If it's tough love
It's tough enough to hold your life
An empty house
An empty daughter and wife
So many found
But not all wished to understand
This is your fate
Your always dealt below the hand
With these last words
I do redeem your only choice
Never again
Will anybody hear your voice.

R Phillips

SHIPWRECK

The captain stood upon the bridge
His eyes were cold in fear
The crew seemed lost, all hope was gone,
Death drew ever near.

So he screamed his orders out
For the crew the ship to save
Many a brave man overboard.
Hit by a mountainous wave.

All hands to the boats he cried
For she's going down
Wrecked upon a mighty reef
On which she has been blown.

Slowly she sank beneath the waves
With the captain on the bridge.
One last salute then he was gone
But in memory, he would still live.

George R Green

A FALLEN MAN

You drink your drink and smoke your dope
For you there is no hope
From my life you have strayed
A decision you have made
They destroy everything that's good
Although you thought they never would
Your giving away your life
The way you gave away your wife
Your boys just wait at the door
Why doesn't daddy come home any more
I tried to stand by you
The way that wives are supposed to do
I've cried and prayed all I can
All for the sake of a fallen man
The path you walk is no good to you
I see the results of what you do
If only you could open your eyes
And stop living all those lies
For your the only one I know
Who could have the strength and just say no
For you are lost, but you could find your way
To live and fight another day.

Elizabeth Leach

PARTING
(In memory of Arthur Edwin Westacott 1914 - 1996)

Tears of a now forgotten sky
Inch into the ceremony as my horror
Hits home of this goodbye, purpled by the
Daimler's purr of entrance.

Inside they come and fidget till
Comfort pacifies their needs of mourn,
Swathed by the musty fragrance of this refuge;
Quiet erupts to the swell of organ pipes
Singing an otherwise inappropriate song of hope.

Then . . . he arrives in the solitude of his gait
Wheeled forward to temporary halt,
So alone but with us and the soprano's stretch
Of voice bathing the fragranced must.

Motionless he remains although we crave
A movement which now will never
Come again; Forced back by the tears of love
He goes onward as the light goes out and the shroud
Of peace envelopes the vision; this must be the sad goodbye.

The one remaining pleasantry of bows to the dead
Falls to the carers who shortly hand him back
For safekeeping of mere minutes; until the ash forms
In the sarcophagi of Thornhill's care.

Yet who would really know where we have been,
For their smiles continue with the bustle of breath
And babies smile now the hiatus breaks free again;
Noise realises its place once more and water flows now for
Remembrance with love.

This is the eternal goodbye . . .

K C Howells

FRIENDS

Friend or foe.
Makes no difference.
To criticise to talk.
But not to think.
The greed of the mind;
Can be hurtful at times.
And should be kept closed;
Lip tight!

Enemy or ally.
People hide behind their own confessions,
What they can not have.
They submit to.
In being hurtful and unkind.
Like a pack of lusting hyenas
They gather together.
And with tongues of spite.
Attack their victims.
Into depression,
And hurt of mind.

Good or bad?
It is too late!
The cast has been set.
The damage is done!
Once there was a friend.
Now there are none.

Carl Hobbs

A GARDEN OF MUSIC

From the banquet hall within
Came the vibrant tones of violin;
It was the soothing rhythm of an ocean breeze
Or the songs of nightingales in the trees.

In a garden of serenity and repose
I wandered to the nearest rose;
In the touch of its petals I could find
Sweet music of another kind:

Fragrance of ecstatic perfume
Drifted forth from every bloom
Drooping tenderly while they sleep.
Silver moonbeams took a peep.

Stars above twinkled in the skies
Scanning the earth with watchful eyes.
This night of splendour, now so still,
Made words easy for the poet's quill.

This beauty all around was mine,
The air intoxicating like a vintage wine.
Like a dream it cannot last
And soon this night will be the past.

The melodies go on till dawn.
The sun will rise, a new day born.
But I am wiser for the night
For I have found a second sight.

There is music in vision as in sound,
In touch and scent it can be found,
And in the taste of sparkling champagne
The violins will play again.

Godfrey Martin

FROM A NEWPORT BAR-ROOM

Rain falls softly and grey in mists as
I gaze out through bar-room window
Into lights lighting for evening's life.
Traffic flows as river does likewise
Under ancient bridge,
Another bridge of time, spanning ages.
I think of you again, wondering,
'Will you ever be mine?'
I ponder and consider
Divination by patterns in beer froth;
'She loves me? She loves me not?'
I order another long drink.

Steve Andrews

ANIMALS

Animals together on this Earth
Who God gave time for them to give birth
Fierce and strong
Mighty and bold
There's always a story to be told
From frogs to ducks
And geese to swans
They are all animals of the pond
Animals from the Amazon Forest
All live there and flourish
I don't see how they could hurt them so
Their so kind-hearted little souls.

K M E Evans

ELEGY FOR A VERY ORDINARY CAT

We loved William,
He wasn't just a cat,
In times of unhappiness
He was scooped up, hugged
And taken to bed,
We scolded him for leaving ginger hairs
On black school uniform,
He ate too much,
Snored,
Sometimes had fleas,
And was old,
Was William.
And then today, a knock at the door,
Did we own a ginger cat?
So sorry, there was nothing he could do
He ran straight out
Did William,
So now I've scooped him up
And brought him to his final bed ,
We've strewn his grave with flowers
We have,
We'll really miss
Our William.

Leila Maryat

MY GRANDAD

We were always together, my grandad and me
There were great things to do, and great places to see.
Forests and rivers and meadows with flowers,
Down country lanes we would wander for hours.

We used to go fishing down by the lake,
Buns, and some sweets, and an apple we'd take
There we'd set sail in our own little boat,
Peaceful and lazy all day we would float.

His garden was famous, all things he would grow
Roses, and dahlias, sweet peas in a row.
His marrows won prizes, his cabbages too,
And he passed on to me all the things that he knew.

I loved my old grandad, and miss him a lot,
And all that he taught me I never forgot,
My own grandchild comes now, and begs me to tell
About all the things I remember so well.

Liz Martin

THERE, THEY'RE, THEIR

They're coming to take me away to-day,
They're coming from over there;
Not from here, but somewhere there:
They're taking me to who-knows-where,
   And I'd really rather stay.

They're saying I have to go away,
They say it'll all be fine.
It may be for their good, not for mine!
And what would happen should I decline
   To go? - I'd make their day.

They'd beat me and bellow Foul Play and say
That I fought them and tore their hair.
I've tried it before, and I'm in despair -
They sought me here and caught me there,
   And wherever I go, they're there.

They're coming to take me away to-day,
And I'd really rather stay.

   . . . Don't say 'There, there'!

Barbara Beaumont

SIR GALAHAD

Sir Galahad Oh valiant knight
Every ladies' swain.
Your blazon standards flight
Your honour and your deeds acclaim.
Your shining armour and crested plume
To many foes these have brought doom.

At tournaments the ladies pray
You wear their favour for the day.
And yet till now through history
Your life is one romantic mystery.
If only you could tell
Which lady held you in her spell.

Christine Williams

JUMP

There are questions to ask and
No answers to give
There is only confusion.
I am shambling through the darkness
With my eyes tightly closed
A sense of total desperation
Comes through these hot stifling tears.

How has it come to this?
Is there hope where there is hopelessness?
Can I ever see the difference?
Can my death become my life?
Shall I fly to a better place
And let God stroke my face
Or will I stay and fight? -

Where is that number 344022
'Samaritans, how can I help you.'

Gail Cureton

LIVE LONGER SAY NO !

In our modern world today
We can no longer plan
A future for our children
That's being destroyed by man.

Drink, drugs and violence
It seems are here to stay
Unless we try to stop it now
They'll take our youth away.

Pushers are at our school gates
Evil men grow rich
Just one tablet is all it takes
To land up in a ditch
Of self destruction and living hell
A shortened life, who can tell.

There will be no tomorrow for some of our very young.
There will be no future in the days to come
Unless we treat pushers as the foe
And have the courage to say *No!*

Joan Watkins

FOR NAN

You are the wind in my face
The sun in my eyes,
You are the nip in the air
The cloud in the skies.

You are the spring in my step
The gleam in my eye,
You are the breath that I take
The tears that I cry.

Carol Mogford

STRANGER IN A STRANGE LAND

Where are you going my foreign friend?
Do you know a road that has no end?
I am searching for it too,
Foreign friend can I come with you?

Will you show me wondrous sights,
Crystal blue waters and bright city lights,
Dazzling sunsets of glowing hue?
Foreign friend can I come with you?

Can you show me temples with statues so tall,
Beautiful icons hung on a wall,
Your people praying to a God so true?
Foreign friend can I come with you?

Could you show me cultures different and new,
Strange little customs known only to you?
Show me your life with a different view,
Foreign friend can I come with you?

With a smile on his face, difference fell apart.
The warmth in his eyes went straight to my heart.
My foreign friend took my hand.
For I was a stranger in a strange land.

Denise Pritchard

THE MONMOUTHSHIRE BRECON CANAL AT FIVE LOCKS PONTNEWYDD

Revitalised stretches, renewed at last,
With waters deep and flowing.
Silvered and shimmering, teeming with fish,
New plant life vigorously growing,
Giving walking enjoyment, and feasts to the eyes,
And a fresh contentment knowing.

Shades of the past haunts the tollpath today
With whispers of voices long dead
Course curses of navvies as they savaged the soil,
Giving it very life as they bled.
The leggers, and lock keepers, stout draught horses
And the ever resounding foot tread.

Years later the calls of we children echoing
And shouting to each other at play.
Sun filled hours of wonder, of newts, frogs, creatures,
Found buried in the thick rich clay.
The minnows and sticklebacks and floating lilies
Carried home lovingly at the close of the day.

Then the tender years of romance and youth
Walking along the path we would go.
Arms entwined, exchanging promises and kisses
Strolling to and fro.
Finding delight in the waters and the banks of green.
As past lovers of long long ago.

Again the sweet smelling scents and sounds
Like the spring at last returning.
Silvered and shimmering again the canal flows,
Beneath the sun so brightly burning.
Giving pleasure once more to both young and old,
Fulfilling at last our hearts yearning.

Anne Whitcombe Sterry

THEIR LIFE

Everyone is alone;
Everyone needs someone;
Everyone has a wish;
Everyone has a hope;
Everyone has a past;
Everyone has a regret.

Some have everything;
Some have nothing;
Some have plenty;
Some have fame;
Some have no home;
Some have no life.

Who knows what will happen to them;
Who knows what they will become;
Who knows how they will survive;
Who knows how they will die.

But they all still need someone;
To love and care for them;
Men, women and children;
The old, the young and the new.

Alison Pearce

RECLAMATION

My valley, O my valley,
Once scared with tips so black,
It makes me so sorry,
As I sit here looking back.

A valley raped of greenery,
Where man was but a slave,
Some found a living,
While others found the grave.

Remove the tips. Fill in the shafts,
Plant trees where trams have been,
Where men once dug for coal,
It's now an ocean of green.

Beautiful my valley now,
And will always be,
Those ugly tips a memory,
Never more to see.

Larry Bowen

THE SILVER STREAM

As I sit here on a style
Musing at the world a while
I watch the swallows flying high
In wonder I give a sigh
To my right a buzzard flying high above
I bet his meal's a collard dove
To my left a grand old hazel tree
Through the middle runs a silver stream
That runs to a river
So fresh and clean
I remember when the river ran black
Waters murky dark and dank
When the mine plumed in the silt and slurry
Then the pit was closed in a hurry
Shouts went out of Oh no and don't worry
Now fish swim in shoals
And birch trees stand bold
Silver birch shimmers and shine like told
But I hear greedy men are in search of black gold
This vision is going to be open cast I'm told.

W H Williams

BUZZARD

On the long plumage of its wings is borne
On the air's ascendancy. Over the stones
Pilloried by time, over the stream's torn
Signature in the earth, almost motionless,
Flies the grim spectacle of its history.
Takes a giant spiral beyond imaginings,
Beyond frontiers, the clock's qualifying
Dictum, the quiet monopoly of its wings
Takes it flying across the dusk, owning to
No specific tenure, scorns the turnpike's
Thin threading out of the hills, With the
Windlass of its bones lifts itself into a
Speck, the firmament of its air space its
Own irretrievable wandering. To see this
Bird sculpted on nothingness, an occasional
Cloud lace dusting it away, drifting,
Drifting into infinity, is like following
The progress of mist over marshland, the
Mire taking into itself the spectre of
Moisture, as the sky's limit destroys a shape
By it distance. Here is a state of being
Remote from the device of the machine, from
Machine-infatuation, an abandonment
To truth, the true state of the free.

Richard Ball

ROSIE

Filter tipped, and bonded.
With each drag,
Drawn together as one.
Yet no carton ever brought nearer
The ties between us, undone.

Lit up, once more from memory,
I carry my tiny torch,
In your name.
Surely, I can stub out
This old flame?

No, secret pleasure
Shared, by your company,
Could ever addict.
They're only leaves,
A taste and tang, of guilt.

So give it up, kick the habit,
Tight lipped, and save your breath.
If we don't inhale, this forbidden
Ash, flicked in the face
Of death.

Will this Adam succumb, tempted,
But out of sight.
Its only absence,
Renews a craving
Yet so deep; I might.

An unholy communion
Still; can't quit
Lest idle hands
Should just reach for another,
Should reach, for you.

M B Chaplin

HUNT

Dark clouds shuffle across a moonlit sky,
As the strigoi out spreads its wings to fly.
This palor gaunt bird hunts only by night,
for naught he fly by the new born'd light.
The branches are out gasping,
The moonlight so shallow.
The mirador inviting,
and the window light mellow,
at the window light tips.
He is nosferatu, dead
He is moroi; full of dread
with those deep deep dark lips
of a deep deadly red.
The hunger now swells him most sure and proud
He has emotion, when it be allowed
Enchanting deep eyes, a glistening red
Stay still now my child, remain in your bed.
The pulse pure emotion wishing him on
Strong winds beating against the window sill
Escaping in to help and free the kill
The prey gasping at breath
Bloody gums suckling death
The end draws on ever closer
The room still looks on, moroser
Till the final curtain, sure and stiff
falls down engulfing, the final kiss
The body is drained and now all is numb
As in a sleeping death what dream will come
For he found prey that soon did die
And all the while the world looked by.

Peter Hall

MARGARET'S GARDEN

Not far from a busy thoroughfare
Must surely be called paradise
A beautiful garden away from public glare
A garden abundant with butterflies
Cascades of flowers tumbling from walls
Exotic wind-chimes echoing their calls
Cheerful pansies swing to and fro
So many colours, setting one's heart aglow
Colourful lizzies staking their claim
All belonging to this hall of fame
Hanging baskets bursting with bloom
Each one special in its own room
Flowers of every description, shape and size
This really is a paradise
Stone squirrels, otters and gnomes
Lifelike and happy in their garden home
A place to retreat to find solace and peace
That's Margaret's garden, where troubles cease.

J Roberts

INNOCENCE OF DUNBLANE

Gone too soon, we don't understand why?
Innocent little angels, that couldn't hurt a fly
Their sweet little faces, so trusting and warm,
Just babes in arms, they'd barely been born.
Sixteen stars in the sky shine bright.
Please Lord protect them all through the night.
No more pain they will feel, no more evil to bear
They'll be safe and looked after in God's loving care
Goodnight little ones, play peacefully forever
And when it's time for you to sleep
Just cuddle up together.

Catherine Wallace

BANISHED

This is the first time I have talked,
About the forest where I once walked.
No one went down there, you see;
But why, was unknown to me.

So I walked down there one summer's night,
Guided by a strange white light.
The light I saw led me deeper and deeper.
The further I went, I grew weaker and weaker.

Then I woke up in a dark, dank place,
With a dim old lamp and kind young face.
She said, 'Don't be scared, please keep calm.
Don't run away; I'll do you no harm.'

And with those last words, she stepped into me.
She found a new host, now her soul could be free.
So with my body, she completely vanished
And here to this day, to this cave I am banished.

Ruth Curtis

WHAT IS A SMILE?

Pleasure or delight or humour
    should it fit
The antidote for quarrel when
    making up a tiff
A greeting for a neighbour

or knowing as a friend

To hide dismay and gloom
While the world goes round the bend.
Everywhere the message each day of the week
But the greatest of them all is from
    the babe who cannot speak!

A J Luke

ROMANTIC RENDEZVOUS

She piled on all her make-up,
Her dress and shoes to match,
She was feeling young and flirty,
Her man would be a catch.

He looked at his reflection,
His shirt was much too tight,
He was feeling fat and forty,
He needed to look right.

She sprayed herself with perfume,
Her nails a brilliant red,
She glanced down at the paper,
She knew what the advert said.

He put on his new jacket,
His tie did not look straight,
He rummaged for his dental floss,
He really felt a state.

She waited for her taxi,
Her head was feeling light,
She quickly glanced to see the clock,
Her timing must be right.

He waited underneath the bridge,
He fiddled with his hair,
He lit another cigarette,
He prayed she would be there.

He stood there for a moment
She smiled and said 'Hello.'
They turned and left together,
The outcome we'll never know.

Helen F Jones

VICTORIA
(For my niece who was still born on May 4th 1990)

A precious little bundle
Was handed to her mother
Wrapped in a hospital blanket,
Her eyes closed as if in slumber.

Her mother cradled her gently,
and stroked her pretty face,
She looked so small, so pretty,
in her bonnet edged with lace.

She gave her to her father
Who held her with pride
Then to her grandparents
Who had been waiting outside

We were not allowed to watch her grow,
to see her start to walk.
Or listen to her babble, when she began
to talk.

We are only left with two photographs
to remind us of that day
We had a lend of Victoria
Before God took her away.

Catherine M Rees

AEGINA MUSE

It's not a bad life, being a Guinea pig
but there again, who wants to be one.
There's not much future being a Guinea pig,
waiting to find out if you're next on the list.
If I come back, I hope I come back as a scientist.

Skelly

IN ABSENTIA

Sunday, and with my leg
still healing, the ramblers go
without me and I sit
staring at the bird
on next door's roof silhouetted
against a leaden sky.

My laptop out of use
I cannot work to fill
the long drear empty days
that weigh upon my heart
since last I heard her voice -
who is not here today.

She comes tomorrow noon
to stay I hope a week
and I shall hold her close
and with that she could stay
but that is not to be
and she's not here *today*

She'd due to ring tonight
three long days since we spoke
and thoughts of her crowd in
intruding on all else
so I can not forget
that she's not here today

E R Kermode

SOLITUDE

Rectangular light,
Sunshine,
Loneliness,
I walk slowly, cautiously.
My emotions become as one.
I'm frozen, I can't move.
The smells of the air become reality.
I sweat with fear.
Fumes of tar and metal surround me.
I can't run I know I'll fall.
I grip the cold harsh metal.
It's my lifeline.
Engines, machinery, shouting.
Sounds that I am used to.
High up above, small birds
Drift, dream, float not a care in the world.
The sounds in the sky make me jump.
But I can't jump.
I'm too scared to move.
Just too scared.
Too scared.
Scared!

Lucy Vincent

SPRINGTIME

In the spring the blossom starts to grow,
As the new sunshine melts the snow,
The coatless lambs start to be born,
The adult frogs lay plenty of spawn.

Beneath the surface of cold, grey mud,
Little green shoots begin to bud,
Evergreens are still bright green,
Yellow daffodils can all be seen.

The delicate crocuses after the snow,
Soon will too, start to show,
The weather forecast shows some rain,
But tomorrow will bring the sun again.

Children play outside all day,
Enjoying their lunch on a picnic tray,
The Easter holidays are such fun,
For the children that is, not for mum.

Gemma Ball

BITTER HOUR

Life is so dark in this, my bitter hour,
My growth is that of a weed strangled flower
Tormented battles they fill up my mind
Sometimes I think that death may be kind
Blackness it comes to fill up my head
Lost is my faith, all I see now is dread
Pieces of me, they fall slowly away
Leaving my life in chaos and disarray
Want to go to heaven, see the warm sun glow
Never again want to see the cold snow fall
Heart so broken can't take back yesterday
Fear for tomorrow, so weary is the way
Panic like poison, that through me spreads
Like winter's season, I'm alive yet dead
Pour me warmth, let it fill up my heart
Bring back the innocence so torn apart
Tears flow, they are constantly shed
Nightmares I see, when at night in my bed
Questions, questions, never any answers found
Like the weed strangled flower, I'll fall to the ground.

Elaine Hawkins

THE UNCAPPED GOWN

Been on my feet since 8 o'clock
By now my feet are steaming hot!
Mother's shouting 'bedroom day'
O how I wish 'twas end of day!
Things are drying on the line,
Suddenly it starts to rain.
Get e'm in, and iron them quick,
The guests are due at half past six.
This lot has got me in a fix!

Carole Smith

UNTITLED

Tiny little hands
Tiny little feet
A perfect little life
A new born baby
Bringing joy to the world
A whole lifetime ahead
The first tooth
The first step
And the first spoken word
A whole host of things
You both discover together
Most of which you've known forever
But a baby brings
New life to all
New meanings to things
You've forgotten
A child can make you
Remember and treasure
The whole world around you.

Tanya Louise Richard

I CAN SEE YOU

I can see you,
Lying there.
You shouldn't be here,
It isn't fair.
Your eyes are glazy,
Pupils fixed.
It's the nets that got you,
The harpoons missed.
I can see you,
Lying there,
You shouldn't be here,
It isn't fair.
They're moving in now,
With knives and shears,
All the townsfolk are moved to tears.
They're slicing, scraping cutting too.
There is nothing I can do.
That's the end
It's over now
There's nothing left
I don't know how,
The rest of you are going to live
We have to help,
And over-run,
The people who killed you
Just for fun.

Tiffany Aubrey

RESOLUTION FOR THE MILLENNIUM

The animals walk in fear of us for our history
    reaches back
Through aeons of thoughtless cruelty to our little
    kinfolk on earth.
The sight of a human being makes each tiny wild
    bird take wing . . .
Yet their parents have to teach them fear.
    It isn't there at their birth.

A cub or a calf, a fledgling or lamb instinctively
    give their trust . . .
Too often betrayed by our actions causing suffering,
    pain and fear.
The time has now come for us all to learn and repay
    their trust with love;
To heal the earth and the animals, and recreate
    Eden here.

Audrey Forbes-Handley

ANGER

Anger is a dreadful thing
In fact it is a mortal sin.
Wasting energy, sapping strength,
Pushes one to any length.
Self destruction, endless pain,
Leaves one thinking,
Am I insane?

Judith Aubrey

KITE

Quicker than the rubbing of the eye
A creature works its wings to fly.
Such tender tissue can only grace
No violence could it satisfy.
Tender is the hook of love,
Love's dawn but an in-drawn wing slow-opened.
I see you as an imposter-something like a kite.

Greta Maclean Jones

THIS IS IT

This is it just wait and see,
Soon there will be less of me,
This time I'll do it there's no doubt,
Inside this fat me, a thin one is trying to get out.

I've bought the leggings, the aerobic tape is set,
Jump up and down till I start to sweat,
My pulse is racing, my face is red,
Hope my heart can stand it I don't want to be thin and dead.

Freeze the chocolates, no biscuits bought,
With this body twenty years I've fought,
Lettuce, tomatoes are all I eat,
Fromage frais a special treat.

I'm lagging now my will power has gone,
I tried for a week but couldn't hold on,
I feel quite sad, why did it have to be,
When God gave out fat he gave most of it to me.

Sue Smith

YES WALES IS A BEAUTIFUL PLACE

Yes Wales is certainly a beautiful place,
where miners once walked to the old pit face.
Singing in unison as they strode to that hole,
unaware they would pay for the *price of coal.*

Working the seams from morning 'til night,
oblivious to the fact of their continual plight.
Proud men had elected to reject the dole,
how could they have known the *price of coal.*

Sirens wailed, it had been a familiar sound,
but alas too late for those buried underground.
In the past the mines had taken their toll,
and all for what, merely the *price of coal.*

For those who survived, some of whom were young men,
now with clogged up lungs, never to work again.
Unwittingly they had worked with body and soul,
regrettably for no more than the *price of coal.*

In the bowels of the earth, now hidden away,
I pray to God it will stay that way.
Yes, the valleys of Wales now play a different role,
since we no longer pay for *the price of coal.*

E M Boyle

DAYS

I go to the Post Office to buy a stamp.
The cold wind bites as along I tramp.
Down a dark gully through a mist of flies
The trees and hedges play at hide the skies

Along the road and past the shop
I'm nearly there I want to hop
Jack Frost has landed on my ears
I wipe my face as I feel cold tears

I go through the door and to the counter
And I have to laugh at the assistant's banter
I'm feeling warmer now, a little better
But go back outside to post my letter

Rotten weather I hear someone call
I turn to see who and walk into a wall
Rotten weather rotten fall
Rotten luck I start to bawl.

C Wiles

HELP SAVE THE ANIMALS

They're taken away from their homes and their families,
Help us to save them, help us, do please.
Why is it done? For the sake of a coat?
They're getting away with it, they can sit back and gloat.

The fur of a fox is all that they need,
But it's a big thing to an animal, so it's still a bad deed.
I wish I could save them, save them all,
Stop fur coats and shawls being sold on any stall.

The poor little animals, show them respect,
And give them the treatment that we would expect.

Kirsty Davies

RED AS A ROSE

Bright the red glow of the glorious rose,
as each petal falls slowly through
wind flows.
It shines with beauty in the sun,
It dances in the breeze, indulging
in fun.
Each delicate petal fades,
Scattering grounds of spring like
flower maids.
A rose dies and goes,
and each tiny, lovely bud grows.

Lianne Futia

THE LOVE SPOON

To her, and only her,
His own beloved future wife,
Young farmer's thoughts across Welsh mountains soar
As on wild falcon's wings
To valley down below.
Then, with rough fingers artistry
His deep devotion is transferred
On to finely-crafted wooden spoon.
Yesteryears' Celtic custom
To carve for sweetheart, still today continues
In creative notches, lines and symbols formed with care.
So what was once dead wood
Will live again to last forever
A token of his steadfast love, passionate and sincere
For her, his *Cariad,*
The darling of his dreams.

Laura Föst

WEATHER IN WALES

Living in Wales
   You may find
That the weather here
   Can't make up its mind

We wake in the morning
   The sky is blue
It's a perfect day
   For a barbecue

We start the barbecue
   The burgers are sizzling
And all of a sudden
   It starts drizzling

The drizzle gets heavier
   It turns into rain
We have to rush everything
   Back inside again

An hour later
   The rain stops
An hour after that
   Down come some more drops

Living in Wales
   You will probably find
That the weather here
   Can't make up its mind.

Anita Ghosh

IDLE GOSSIP

I overheard in the grocer's
Some awful conversation,
And a cold accusation
About Mrs Price.
Nancy Thomas and Sheila Smith
Accused her of being rude -
Nancy Thomas is a prude.
I like Mrs Price.
They said she'd spoken out of line
When asked about her daughter,
And the china she'd bought her.
She'd never do that.
They shouldn't have been so nosy
As that's her business, not theirs -
Meddling into her affairs.
It's just idle chat.
Mrs Price has a heart of gold
She bakes me blackberry pie;
With a twinkle in her eye -
Scrumptious I might say.
I don't really care what they say
I know that none of it's true -
They've nothing better to do -
Than gossip all day.

Helen Deborah Bennett

ROSES ROUND THE DOOR

When I was but a boy and young
To my mother's home I clung
And her cottage windows smiled
When up the weary hill I toiled.
The welcome there was always sure,
To all who needed - rich or poor
And who were greeted there
By roses round the door.

Now I am old and full of care
My own front door stands proudly there,
My loves have come, my loves have gone
And someone else enjoys the sun.
Once in a while my spirits soar
when to my God I implore,
'Take me where, there will ever be -
Roses round the door.'

Marjorie Scott

SILENT LOVER

Infinity of suppressed desire
Senses maimed, emotions sealed.
Forbidden passion, the spark to the fire
Time was supposed to, instead never healed
That ache of bereavement, that nag in her chest
As she clasped those memories that ignited her soul
Symptoms of loss left to manifest
In her world now transformed to an empty
Black hole.

Claire Lovell

SMALL

Pinhole star
Universal shine,
Do you see me?

I believe I am like you:
Lonely and cold,
Insignificant too.
But do I shine as bright
In my dark sky?
Indifferent to the light,
And its absence outside.
If your maker created me also,
Then why place me
Such a distance below?
For you are clean and pure and sweet,
Like everything good
Always out of reach.

Richard Reid

PERFECT

What right have you got to say,
That I should look a certain way.
Why should you dictate my height,
Or say I should have no cellulite.
What difference does it really make,
If my bust is real or fake.
Or if my bum is tight as hell,
Why can't it be a flabby shell.
My body shape I will not change,
We should be accepted across the range.
So, I'll never pay a hefty fee,
To change myself, I will be me.

M Pickering

TEARS OF LOVE

My heart is broken,
the pain is so great,
I try to turn my love into hate.
Alone in my sorrow,
I dread each tomorrow.
My heart is bleeding,
the pain is so great,
I try to turn my love into hate.

I know that I'm sinking,
each day is too late.
the love that I'm loosing,
can't seem to wait.
Love has invaded the depths of my soul
and the price to pay is taking its toll.
The tears that I cry are tears of love,
but they don't wash away the pain.

Josephine Bottino

VERY LIKE OGDEN NASH

Somebody once dared Ogden Nash to write a poem with the word
Monosodiumglutamate in it
And Ogden Nash said 'That's not really so very hard
Because if you write the sort of so called poetry I write
You can say almost anything you like
And people will think you're a bit of a card:
For example, I could just as easily decided to write a poem
Using words like gargoyle and coagulate
Then, just for the hell of it, I'd find some really silly rhymes for them
Like cod liver oil or monosodiumglutamate.'

G Jones

LIVING ON A GRANT CHEQUE

My life has changed, now I'm a student.
I've certainly become much more prudent
with my affairs in the world of money
- there's no more living on milk and honey.

My grant is frugal, to say the least.
No more luxuries do I feast.
No longer I dine on succulent roasts,
but more often now on beans on toast.

When I am invited out
I often hear my wallet shout
'Leave me alone, I won't go far!
You'll have to raid the penny jar!'

I pass the High Street boutiques by
- it's jumble sales that get me high.
Two pounds a coat, fifty pence a top
When I've spent five pounds I have to stop.

My plastic wallet has been with me
through thick and thin - well, thin, mainly.
There's much more cloth than cold, hard cash.
I don't have any notes to stash.

My overdraft looks like a telephone number,
though how it got so high I can't remember.
Despite all this, I know I'll pull through,
as tomorrow, my next grant cheque's due.

Julie A Kinnair

DOWN A HARDENED RUT

I scarcely saw that throbbing tractor pulling bales of hay,
For on this cart-track came the horse wain of a former day,
Full superposing, swaying, creaking, with Seth Baines on foot,
Who led fly Daisy to the rickyard down a hardened rut;
A sound of leather chafing leather, then a snorting blow,
A sound of crunching iron rims I hear, as on they go,
Their load high up above the hedge, young Sam and Joe on top,
Who'll have this last lot ricked and tightly thatched before they stop.

Long quiet hours of patient labour quenched with ginger ale,
Good meals around the farmyard table, everybody hale,
And proud of everything they did . . 'tis grand to walk this way,
Where merry fellows pitched from dawn a scented field of hay;
And Daisy, broad and strong, was steady - if a trifle vain -
She knew the way of it alright when harnessed in the wain
Unhurried, holding back to turn an arc below each gate,
Nor bothered if, to clear the field, there was an extra weight.

That's how it was. The tractor passed, eleven for his load,
Two rows of four with three above, along the same old road,
Its acrid smell of diesel smoke would spoil that lovely scent
Of honeyed swath, as through my muse those former workers went;
But there the field . . . and there a sun just as it was before,
Eight acres cleared . . . a winter fodder guaranteed once more,
Perhaps not quite so happy even then, if I might say,
As when Seth Baines with Sam and Joe had cut that golden hay.

The Warwickshire Poet

THE EAGLE

In context, eye through windscreen window
swooping effortless and mean
from lower to upper chapel
the old derwen stands
surrounded by
nothing.

The army of occupation trundles up to Sennybridge,
acnied, hackneyed troops, map reading and muttering.
From here, the lorry dots scurry like vermin,
Talons stretched like creaking tarpaulin,
I swoop.

Many, long gone from here now, of the very bloodied earth
we vilify, turn gently over.
The worms disdain to appear.
Anorexic sparrows hobble and peck,
I swoop.

Cilmeri stands silent, Obelisk glinting flashes of hope
despite the pungent smell of diesel exhaust.
Small buds appear, autumnal droplets feed and refresh.
Sprouting, moving, growing.
Then trampled by a black, buffed boot.
I swoop.

Dafydd Williams

THE PRISONER

Your little home is much too small,
You've scarcely room to fly at all,
Poor 'budgie' in your gilded cage,
It often makes me burn with rage,
To see you in that awful prison,
When to the heavens you may have risen.

Garnet Hoddell

SAVE NOT KILL

By polluting the planet, and skies above,
We kill the world that we should love.

We kill the trees that give us air,
And all the creatures who live there.

No place have wild life left to run,
It's either an axe or a farmer's gun.

All God's creatures have no say,
It's man who thinks he knows the way.

What a mess he's made so far,
Just more roads to drive his car.

A concrete world without no trees,
With toxic pollution in our seas.

We have to change before to long,
Or this planet may be gone.

Jayne Pearce

BLUEBELLS

Jangling and tangling
falling on the floor,
People taking pictures standing at the
door,
One string connecting ten flowers
They keep on growing for hours and hours,
Jingle jangle as they blow
Hoping that you will not go.

Anna Jackson-Scott

LONG SUMMER DAYS

Long summer days
Early morning heat haze
Meadow sweet and clean country air
Cows that stand and stare
Blushing poppies in a field
Birds singing their praises
Fresh sandy shore
Chestnut mare along the bay
Rider in his coat of grey.

Deep hush in the countryside
Sleepy cottages awake
Farmer working with his rake
Housewife's laundry on the line
Cat on doorstep looks sublime
Hungry herons on the wing
Soaring seagulls overhead
Rock pools glistening in the sun
Grim faced cliffs look out to sea
Ocean moving perpetually
Salty air and fishing smacks
Footprints deep in sanded shore
A rusty trumpet sounds no more.

Audrey Adsett

THE STORM

I sit and watch the clouds,
They gather with such force,
Their power is all consuming,
Nature will take its course.

The lightning flashes all around,
The palm trees bend and sway,
The sky is threatening, angry now,
The storm's not far away.

The rain begins to fall,
In sheets of shining glass,
The thunder rumbles overhead,
But it will quickly pass.

The lightning fades, the thunder too,
And all is calm once more,
The trees are still, the air is fresh,
And all is as it was before.

Diana Jackett

1966

In the morning the mist hugs the valley and it
cloaks the hilltops.
The darkness is dying as the morning is
born.
Villagers awaken under the brightness.
But the terraces are over shadowed by their
cold sadness.
The men continue to work in the coal mine,
The women work in the homes,
And the children play in the back streets.
Wheels of labour slowly and reluctantly grind
on.
Machines and industry revolve and his
feelings become deeper.
His watch seems to turn backwards as time
passes so slowly.
Housewives grow weak and weary.
But the children's energy is never ending.
They attempt in vain to play games, try to
ignore the grief that surrounds them.
The miner's joy in returning home is lost
forever.

David Sheppard

I DO BELIEVE

Sometimes you have to be,
More than a hero, more the fool,
The victim and the sacrifice.
Sometimes you have to risk it all
Or face defeat,
Knowing that the odds,
Are stacked way-up-too high.
      But still you try
      And I do believe,
      Someday you will learn to fly.
      Yes you try
       And I do believe,
      Someday you'll learn to fly.

Sometimes you have to be.
More than the hero, more the fool,
The victim and the sacrifice.
Sometimes you have to watch the dream
Just slip away,
Into the lonely night,
Where all the hopes and fears take flight,.
      And still you try
      And I do believe,
      Someday you'll learn to fly.
      Yes you try
      And I do believe,
      Someday you'll learn to fly.

C Sumner

LOOK AROUND

I look around at life and think
What is it really for?
We have our ups, we have our downs,
We live through peace and war.
And like the tide washes up the beach
And bursts its many bubbles.
We have to cope throughout our life
With lots of little troubles.
But, look around, young babes are born
Who'll never take your hand,
Nor play at making castles
On the sunny golden sand.
So, you out there, be thankful
For what you've really got.
Look around, be happy
And appreciate your lot.

Lucy Hartley

THIS CHILD OF MINE

When you came into the world
I cried with joy
At last my own baby boy
I no longer feel sad or broken in two
Life seems worth living at last for you
You gave me courage you gave me strength
The meaning of life makes much more sense
There are no more doubts they are all gone
For you now I must be strong.
I must get on with living every day
For you my child it's the only way
And while you are sleeping I look down at you
My own fair angel my wish has come true.

Marcia Bailey

TURNING TIDES

Oh rolling waves, tempestuous sea,
You bring me peace, tranquillity.
Especially when you are calm and still,
I close my eyes, relax at will.
Now revealed is the golden sand
Where those in love walk hand in hand.
Lonely walkers, words unspoken,
Who's to know their heart is broken?
As daytime slowly turns to night
It's peaceful here and oh so right.
I close my eyes but I still see
A better place I could not be,
To warm my soul and clear my mind
That's the feeling I will find.
Kaleidoscope patterns with every tide,
Great creator ocean wide.

Phil Williams

ACCESS DAY

Sunday, the park is cold, the January air bites through our clothes.
So many lonely dads with no place else to go.
Angry and confused without the life they've known,
while their mother's snug and warm in the house that once was home.
Missing the security of that life they used to share
He fights to keep the love alive for the children in his care.
Barred from the door that used to welcome him each day,
cold and sad he takes them to the park of yesterday.
Memories of sunny hours, moments they would share, now he fights
to hide the tears from the little ones close there.
He wants so much to share their love, not for just a day,
but has to settle for the freezing park,
there's nowhere else to play.

E V

MY SEASIDE DAY

I jumped out of bed and smiled with glee,
As I gazed out the window to look at the sea.
The seagulls were squawking up in the sky,
Dodging each other as they gracefully fly.

I put on my costume and picked up my bag,
I threw in a towel, bucket, spade and a mag.
I jumped down the steps and onto the sand,
I tied back my hair in a big scrunchy band.

I left on the sand my bucket and spade,
And into the water I started to wade.
I laid on my back and started to float,
And far out to sea was a huge fishing boat.

I then picked up my things and went back to my flat,
And when I went in I let out the cat.
Then in the night when I went up to bed,
I dreamt of my day going round in my head.

Laura Anne Evans

THE MOTORBIKE

With straining cog, and speeding chain, with swirling wheel, and
bucking main.
On upward hill, or downward dale, my pipes sing out there blanching
wail.
A tyre, to tear the tarmac road, a tank, my living blood to hold,
a spark within, a throb of life.

With wind on face, like needled ice, I am for youth the thrill of speed,
so aptly named, the fiery steed.

K R Lamprey

GRATITUDE

No it's not what you have;
In terms of money.
You can keep all your
    Status and wealth.

The things that I value,
    Money can't buy.
'Tis the air that I breath,
    And my health.

I've nothing in envy.
Of all well to do.
    There's merit for gold,
In one's purse.

But each in its order,
And purpose the day.
Brings contentment
To all souls on earth.

No maps yet completed,
Show this treasure trove find.
    Of contentment,
And peace every day.

The enigma of life,
Is a puzzle no more.
    If in gratitude

We praise and pray.

Windsor Hopkins

THE CAUSE

Collar up, black cap drawn close
down over the eyes, shielding the
soul. The walk, shoulders as your
grandfather in the bone; mutter,
reactionary, revolutionary: appeal to
this anarchist, hiding narrow,
in alcoves of self. Tempted to seek
secrets, revealing enough to
catch you, watch you, slipping
through the hot shadows of
towns: chase you in a dream, think
you in conflict. The cause?
Join you in the cause; revolution,
revelation. Wait. Resolution.

L A Churchill

ECO WARRIORS

The Fort of Trollheime
Stands high upon the hill
With eco warriors
All standing still
Waiting for the guards
To come they defend
Our land to stop the
Destruction of this our
Place we live the
Fort of Trollheime will
No longer stand when
They have won this
Battle but they won't
Win only eco warriors
Left to defend our
Land and fight another day.

Bob Lewis

AT THE STATION

'The train due to arrive at eight o'clock
Will now arrive at eight-fifteen.'
A disembodied voice booms out
From somewhere hidden in the roof.
With sighs and groans of disbelief
A dozen travellers adjust their lives:
The smart executive, briefcase in hand,
Gets out his papers and begins to work -
A daily happening for him;
The rough and ready type with muttered oath
Snorts down his mobile to his mate.
Two grey-haired grannies, neatly dressed,
Complain about the state of things;
Young lovers hold each other close,
Ignorant of all around;
While school children, with shouts of glee,
Play tag and dodge from post to post.
Two long-haired lads slump in their seats
Prepared to catch up on some sleep
And Mr Smith nags at his wife:
They should have left an hour ago!
A crackling and that nasal voice again:
The train arrives; the tensions lift
And all is harmony once more.
The platform stands deserted now
Except for one lone, tearful girl
Who waves her boyfriend out of sight.

Kathleen Wendy Jones

DAYBREAK

The forest slept
Cradled by dawn's pearly mist
Silent, peaceful
Suddenly golden arrows pierced the trees
Darting, darting
The sun rose in all its splendour
Banishing the mist
The forest stirred
Whisperings, stirrings
The call of a bird in flight
The morning breeze stirred the lake
The forest was awake.

Eileen Hollins

LUXURY

Comfortable in your own home,
Fully furnished,
Velour three piece,
Matching curtains,
Ever so . . . neat.

But you don't match the colour scheme,
It's not ideal.
You don't match the colour scheme,
Because you are real.

It's an odd situation,
You are the only thing that's not imitation.

In your dream home,
Suburban show home,
Deck chair. Pond. Garden gnome.

Darren Snaith

THE FURY OF NATURE

Storm clouds straddle wooded mountains,
Rain lashes down on banks of pine,
Winds howl and scream in jagged canyons,
All nature's powers intertwine.

Long shafts of energy pierce the sky,
Lighting up primeval scenes,
Savage elements dance with fury,
Man dare not cannot intervene.

White waters rushing headlong downwards,
Gathering strength with every yard,
Pounding, breaking, swiftly snaking,
Damaging all with disregard.

And while tempests rage in frenzy,
Man stands afraid and trembling,
Nature wields her awesome weapons,
Free, unchecked and menacing.

When at last storms run their course,
Man creeps out to face the dawn,
Mountains now are tinged with sunlight,
The Earth smells clean and newly born.

Inas Everett

THE DOOR

   What's behind this door,
What secrets does it hide,
   if I opened this door right now,
I *wonder* what I'd find.

   What's behind this door,
what stories could it tell,
   why is this door so big,
and, why does it look so . . . well?!

I can't see a keyhole,
but I wouldn't mind a step,
   because, only being *five* years old,
I can't reach the handle yet!

   What's behind this door,
I can't wait to see,
   but first I'll have to grow a bit,
and *finally* I'll see.

K Grady

MY TAID

My Taid was always telling jokes,
He liked to make everyone laugh,
He used to go for little strolls,
Up the garden path.

He used to joke about what I wore,
And also about my hair,
Until in the end he would stop joking,
And sit quietly in his chair.

But then he became very ill,
And started to forget things,
I like to remember him as he was before,
When he would laugh and sing.

Now he's gone forever,
But he'll always be in our hearts,
We'll all remember him as funny and kind,
With his bitter and his farts.

It's time for me to start anew,
And carry on as I did before,
But always and forever he'll be there in my mind,
And my heart which is now sore.

Claire Thomas (13)

SPRING

The majestic morning,
Bejewelled with dew,
Misty,
Mystical,
Born anew,
Before man has rudely awakened
The day with noise,
And shaken the dew with crude
Footsteps.
Oh to be out there,
To bless the earth,
And kiss the grass,
Bathe in dew,
To run wild in the wind
Free spirit,
Born anew.

Sian Boissevain

PERSONAL FIX

Blank stares - luminous in display,
bright flickering thoughts,
shivered my approach mere inches away;
Where does it lead me?
Hear silence beneath electric hiss,
created from another's vision
of time in motion - in motion still
changing images float past.
Deny their power; transported
to another year, imagination's tricks
entice into dream worlds.
I am in opposition to my friend and foe.

Janet Dalmar

THE SAD MOUNTAINS

In the north,
Mist mantled
Cloud crowned
Silent in majesty
Lasting eternity
Towers sad Snowdonia.

Drenched in nature's tears,
Stonily brooding
Quietly mourning
Waiting willingly
Hoping helplessly
Snowdonia waits in vain

Ringed by Edward's castles,
Towering impregnable.
Staying unconquerable
Llewellyn they guarded
They, Llewellyn failed
Waiting eternity, sad Snowdonia

In the misty north,
Impassive and sad
Grey and cold
Quietly awaiting
Llewellyn's return,
Waiting in vain
Eternally mourning
Towers sad Snowdonia.

Kevin Bratherton

SOMETIMES

Sometimes, I wonder if I have lived before, because
when I look out of my front door I remember when this
place was all coalmines and dust.
Whereas now it is green.
I remember that I have seen men walking to work
carrying the tools of the mining trade; but that's long gone now.
And I remember putting my hand up to my brow and bidding
'good morning' to the rising sun as it rushes up the valley.

Sometimes, I remember battles with our English leaders,
but now we only fight on the grass of the Arms Park, or if we
lose the draw we play at their grounds.
There is nothing better in this whole world than hearing the
sounds of the Welsh as they sing our anthem.

Sometimes, I am amazed how time goes by; how the minutes and
hours and days fly:
Next year I shall be seventeen.
At night I look out over the dusky green and
remember what has gone before.
Lord, before you lay my soul to rest, take this life with which
I have been blessed,
I ask just one thing of you:
Let my memories live on even though I am through.

The sun may shine in America, Australia and the rest,
but the green of the valleys is what I love best.
Sometimes, just sometimes, I wish I could roam.
But I know in the end I will return home.

Keri L Thomas

AND DID THOSE FEET?

When Jesus went to Merthyr,
To Zoar and to Zion,
He blessed the 'nymphs of Glebeland,'
And cursed the men of iron

When Jesus went to Newport,
He went to 'stand and stare'
At overburdened shoppers,
So pale and full of care

When Jesus travelled westward,
The Saints were filled with malice,
He stayed at Govan's Chapel,
Instead of Bishop's Palace

When Jesus went to Swansea,
His look was 'Bible-black',
On graveyard of ambition
For King and Queen - and Jack!

When Jesus went to Brecon,
He saved them from their sin,
He opened up the gates, and now
The Saints Go Marching In!

When Jesus came to Cardiff,
He went to Cardiff Bay,
He shed a little teardrop,
And then he went away!

P J Davies

COLOURING MY COUNTY

Spring in my county,
Colours are new.
Mother nature mixes,
Her pastels with dew.

She fills up her brush,
And with one stroke of hand.
She colours my county,
The best in the land.

Summer in my county,
Colours are vast.
Mother nature empties,
Her pallet quite fast.

She colours the flowers,
To enhance the greens.
Crowning my county.
The king amongst queens.

Autumn in my county,
Colours are few.
Mother nature ponders.
Then decides what to do.

She colours the greens,
With rust mauve and brown.
Her pallet's almost empty,
She places it down.

Winter in my county,
Colours are two.
Mother nature paints,
With snow white and ice blue.

She covers my county,
In a blanket of white.
Then sprinkles on ice blue,
Until the shimmer's just right.

She stands back admiringly,
When her pallet's all spent.
For she loves as I do,
My own county Gwent.

Frances Griffiths

TEMPUS FUGIT

Whither went those halcyon days
Before I entered the twenties' maze?
When summer was long and full of light
And the world revolved for my delight.

A tiny lessening of evening sun
There seemed when I reached twenty-one;
And when I'd thirty summers seen
The fields, and I, were both less green.

A forty, life was racing by.
I had a somewhat jaundiced eye
For folk who said 'Don't make a fuss -
Life *really* begins at forty-plus.'

At fifty they said I was at my peak
Though the bloom had long since left my cheek.
But now the evening sun grows cool
And I know myself for a life-long fool.

A life-long fool with death at my side
Mid the wrecks of my youthful dreams that died.
Now my faults and follies rise grim and stark
To haunt me till my world grows dark.

R Roberts

OUR FAIR LAND

Dragons, harps, leeks, scenes,
Cawl, cakes, farms, dreams,
Daffodils, tea, village shops,
Seaside, countryside, mountain tops,
Rugby, friendly, singing, dales.
All these things you'll find in Wales.

Dawn Ridler

LAND O'SPIRITS

O'er yonder skies far away
The sun dawns another day,
Living things, wild things all around,
In the sky, upon the ground
O'er the midst we fail to see
The man, the friend, the Aborigine.

For in this man lies a past
Also a present, a future to cast,
Living, learning we do, to find our culture too;
Observe this spirit the land of hope
Floating, guiding, helping us to cope.

Searching for this peace of mind
This guiding spirit it hard to find,
These men are our hope for peace and joy,
That all began from a little boy.

That lost forgotten tribe, in spirit will survive,
The bush echoes with didgeridoos
Kookaburras and kangaroos:
'Hark' the sound of whispers in the trees
Tells us that our world of man will never cease.

R Maskill

SUMMER A WALK AT DUSK

Dusk was taking his turn of the day
the golden sun had given him way,
So up on the hillside for a quiet stroll
to see more or nature's secrets unfold.
There stands a tree, a sturdy beech
its trunk has been hollowed by time
living inside are bats of the night
so high they are out of reach,
Beech mass in clusters hang from its arms.
Hawthorn with berries surround the farms,
Through the ferns as I walk
flutter shiny leaves
small and silver fritillaries.
A rest in a clearing not far from a brook
on a hill as I sit and
there in a nook
lovely flowers pretty blue hues
I took my breath to pay them my dues
their spurred petals arranged like doves
each drooping azure blue of love.
Someone named them columbine
a sweet name like a bell that chimes,
Overhead swifts fly close and free
so close they could almost touch me.
What a perfect time to visit nature
before she ebbs to slumber,
Visions I see of glorious scenes
are far too rich to number.

Jacquie Williams

TEARS OF LOVE

And he looked into the
eyes of Venus, and she
wept for him before
extracting his empty and
unfulfilled soul.

As the slave of pain and
suffering fell to his knees,
cries of anguish and
mourning echoed
throughout the palace.

Venus rose back up into
the sky with the soul of
the slave still pulverising
in her grasp.

Venus thought for a
moment before releasing
the slave's soul to the
people of the world.

David Thomas

STREET VENDOR'S HYPERBOLE

Dreary you may think it
to wend your weary way
a-dragging of your footsteps
straight past my vendor's dray;

But if you wish to place a smile
upon your faces fair
I'm just the aphrodisiac
to make your day, so there!

Please stop awhile, and think on
my juice upon your lips
to tempt your ever-loving
to reach out for your hips;
he'll think of eastern promise
as he carries you to bed . . .
please buy me, lovely ladies,
I'm a bloody orange - *red!*

Douglas M Henly

THE CALLER AT THE OLD INN'S DOOR

I would see him in the pale moonlight
Riding over the old coastal road,
With swish of cloak around him
To mask his purpose more,
And face dashed against the wild wind
To thoughts upon the shore.

And I would hear him by rook's corner
Whispering at the old inn's door,
To the creaking of the sign above
Yet I never caught his name,
Only the rush upon the night's air
And his urgent need to gain.

And the hurried roll of the barrel
Across the stained cobbled floor,
The impatient champ of his horse's hoof
Upon the courtyard's lawn,
The clink of foot back into iron loop
And then he was gone.

Norman Royal

AMBITION

Ambition - it is, that old fateful flaw,
you get a taste of it and then you want more.
It burns, it breeds deep within your soul,
and makes you do *anything* to achieve your goal.

You use people like garbage and then throw them away,
you take pleasure in ruining everyone's day.
You're out of control, you're power mad,
you lose all the friends that you once had.

It's taken over, you blackmail, you conspire,
- burning within you this unquenchable fire.
You lose all your morals, your dignity, your pride
you've got what you wanted, who cares that you lied?

Ambition - it should be one of the deadly sins,
for when it envelopes you, it takes over and wins.

David Wederell

TIME

Time flows on,
Constantly, no going back,
Leaving only memories
Ebbing tides of misery, disappearing into the past.

The future arrives,
The present we live through.
Hard at the time, but disappears
Back into nightmares and dreams.

Plans ripped asunder,
A cut of the knife, rips apart the threads of life,
But time carries on, no halting the black sands of time
Then golden grains emerge as
                      Time flows on.

Anne Jones

AND TELL ME

Stars and space, light years of endless grace,
Beckoning onward the seamless past.
Dead men sailing heaven's vaults looking on aghast!
Didst Man's courage fail him then?
Is this the reason why, in all the heart's adventures,
the soul-destroying lie.
The grail is gone forever! We cannot search anew
and, told the quest is over, anoint the craven few.

So tell me! Who placed iridescence upon these
                                        grey men's scales?
And exchanged it for a colder hue beside which,
                                        nought avails.
And tell me! In their endless sheet of profit against loss,
where do they find their bloodless strength to kneel
                                        amid the dross?
I curse and damn these scoundrel fools for stealing history,
for holding golden rainbows, in chains of misery.

But is the dream that once was thine burning brightly still?
Held in heaven's rapture that men might look their fill.
It is still there, that much is clear, flaming from afar,
the heartbeat quickens swiftly when gazing on a star.
Throw off thy chains, come! Launch thy craft,
let's search for mighty things.
For when we seek our destiny, 'tis then that heaven sings!

Colin Davies

WHY?

Why? Why did you leave?
I felt so alone.
Why did you leave us?
Leave us on our own!

We were, oh! So little
so small and defenceless.
Why did you leave us?
It really was senseless!

My brother was only five years old,
and I was only eight.
I waited, hoping you'd come back,
I waited by the gate.

Night after night, I waited.
I sat by the phone,
waiting for you to call
To say you're coming home.

That was twenty years ago
But still, I sit and wait
longing to see you
Walk through my open gate.

C A Edwards

BOSNIA (THE BLUE BERETS)

Bosnian heroes, with berets of blue,
Doing their best, to see a job through,
The fight is not theirs, but there they must be,
To try and bring peace, to this war-torn country.

The children, follow food lorries for miles,
Hopeful faces, with tears and smiles,
The tears are plenty, the smiles are few,
The men in blue berets, they sometimes cry too.

Children in rags, with hands out to greet,
The blue beret hero, who comes with a treat,
This country, once proud, decided to die,
People went crazy, we'll never know why.

Round tables, square tables, the powers that be,
Sit around squabbling, for the right to be free,
Leaders of men, and politicians,
Representing all, the United Nations.

Nations united? It doesn't seem right,
That neighbours, once friendly, suddenly fight,
And through all this, working night, working day,
Are the heroes that wear the blue beret.

Middy

THE LONELY OLD MAN

A lonely old man
Sits alone in his chair
Wondering to himself
Does anyone care?

Nobody visits him
Yet he waits on
Hoping that someone
Will come along.

But all his visitors
Stay at home
And the lonely old man
Dies alone.

Natalie Bennett (Age 15)

DOWN IN THE DELL

Down in the dell where the fairies flit,
There might be something you've given a miss.
The down of the dandelion circling by.
The new born butterfly attempting to fly,
Caterpillars creep in the woodland leaves.
Mice dash around to feed their yealdes.
The glistening sun through the tops of the trees
giving radiance to the bright green leaves.
Still damp with dew of the night,
the mushroom heads come up with delight.
The woodland flowers show up, here and there,
a scatter of colour everywhere.
The nightingale goes in flight, on wing,
then settles again and starts to sing.
How nice to go down to the dell again,
It's just at the end of that narrow lane.

Geraldine Ward

REALITY

Welcome to reality, welcome to today,
We know there's not much hope for us,
No matter what they say.
Welcome to racism, prejudice and pain,
say hello to pollution, smog and acid rain.

Welcome to the future,
although it seems so bleak.
Full of petty wars and murder,
someone's dying as we speak.

Welcome our generation,
of drug addicts and boozers.
Welcome to tomorrow,
a world that's full of losers.

Claire Taylor

DECISION

I look around and what do I see?
A chance in a million, just waiting for me.
Should I jump and take it now?
Or sit back and wonder, pondering how,
How will it change me?
What will I miss?
Am I quite ready, up to all this?
I treasure the life I've already got.
I don't want to lose that, no I do not.
But look at this new road, directed at me,
A world of adventure, daring and free.
Should I be happy?
Should I be sad?
Or should I just take it,
Carefree and glad.

Debra Greenhouse

MAN'S BEST FRIEND

The best friend I
Ever had, would sit there looking
Very sad,

Until I touched her
On the head, and told her it was
Time for bed,

She would wag her tail
And grab her lead,

And jump on my lap and
Plead and plead,

Alright I give in, I'll take
You for a little spin,

Just around the block I
Would say, and she would look at
Me as to say OK,

She would run and roll
In the park,

And chase squirrels until
It got dark,

Then home again we would
Walk, having a quiet little
Talk,

Open fire and soft settee,
My friend would sit just
Her and me.

Laurence Mann

PHYSICALLY MEASURABLE

The sun has cracked your face
Cruelly, split the visage
A slab of cheese, hardened
By exposure, yellowed and divided.
A foot that has walked too many a mile
From a hurt that is too large
For any love of mine
To be able to replace.

Karen Newsham

RAIN

What a wonderful thing is rain,
It falls on the roof and down the drain,
Into the rivers, down to the sea,
It moistens the air making it fresh
                            with the breeze,
Helping the farmers to grow good crops,
After tilling the land when it was dry and hot,
Reaping their harvest, taking it to towns,
Being rewarded in crowns.

How would we have managed without
this miracle from heaven called rain.
We'd have shortage of water,
Droughts, grass would turn brown,
Nothing would grow the same,
So when we hear sounds of rain falling
on the roofs, down the drains,
into the rivers, down to the sea,
we can all rejoice once again,
for this watering of the land
is pure nature and free.

Leighton Haigh Edwards

WHO NEEDS LOVE?

Everybody has somebody.
All apart from me.
Like a pebble washed up on the beach
refused by the waves of the sea.

Love stalks and hunts its victims,
ignoring my small plea,
leaving me all alone,
locking my heart with its key.

Everyone else a couple,
a twosome, a duet.
Me, a blackbird amongst the lovebirds.
A loser on love's roulette.

Waves crash on my empty heart.
Empty of warmth and love.
While sweethearts bask in a sea of hope.
With my longing stare from above.

And as I sit on my cliffs of woe,
I stare out at the sea.
Wondering is it all worth it?
And surely it's not just me?

What is this love?
Jealousy, fear and pain?
Wondering if he'll love you back
or on your heart will rain.

If love is just unhappiness,
insecurity, fear and misery.
I'd rather be in school my dear,
doing homework and in history!

Deborah C Jones (14)

PROGRESS

How green lies the valley
How beautiful the dawn
Free of the master's industry did spawn.
No furnace heat or flame
No belching fire or steam
No roar or crashing steel
in coil, or sheet that gleam.
To herald ghostly claim
come clinking, clanking chains
for man, his fate to seal.

Pit wheels still and idle
where man was once a mole
burrowing on his belly epitaph to coal.
No more winding cages
No more choking dust
No more digging tunnels
only bogies left to rust:
And, sheep graze on coaltips now green.

One may argue that a miner
will live a longer life
breathe without the rasping pain
that cuts him like a knife.
True to say is every word
but bear in mind man's soul,
closing down all industries
make master of the dole . . .
When man believed the story
that progress was sublime,
no-one dared to count the cost
till man was bade, goodbye.

Shirley Silman

THE SWING

Swing higher and higher into the sky,
see the clouds floating by;
closer ever closer to thee
if only dear sister it could be.
You are in my thoughts each day
and always when I pray.
You are to me still seven
as no-one grows older in heaven.
To swing again together
just for a time, not forever;
I would give this day to you.
For yours on Earth were too few.
Swing higher and higher into the sky,
we did not even say goodbye.
I know you will wait be it ever so late,
so that we may swing together.

Pauline Davies

NOW

Don't leave it too late,
To say that you care,
Because you're shy to relate,
'Glad you are there.'

Life comes only once,
If you miss just a day,
You will always wish,
For words of yesterday.

So say them all now,
And look for the smile,
Telling how much,
They are worthwhile.

Susan Green

THE STORM

The wind it blew, on that hot summer's night,
the sky went dark: there's a storm in sight.
Look out over the Dee, to the Wirral and beyond
the sea's as calm as a calm mill pond.
The thunder claps the rain does pour
the lightning strikes like I've never seen before,
the sea has changed it's rough and wild.
It's not fit for any man, woman or child.
The lightning strikes just one more time.
It takes out the electricity and the telephone line,
the children look and stare in surprise,
as the TV goes off before their very eyes.
What do we do now; you hear them say
there's lots of games that we can play,
but there's no electricity, how do we see.
We'll light a candle or maybe three.
We played some games, and had lots of fun.
Then the storm it finished just like it begun,
with a loud clap of thunder
then out came the sun.

Dariann Sealby

BLIND, DEAF AND EXCEPTIONALLY DUMB!

I call you my 'pain of parting' man,
I'm practised at it so I really can
Stand as authority on this fact:-
That you are a fool
and always will act
in a way that is stupid,
as when you'd the chance,
you mistook someone else
for your 'life's real romance.'

Sylvia Pollard

MY SPORTING SON

100 metres, discus, shot,
bowls and javelin too,
table tennis, basketball,
all these sports my son can do.

Competes in competitions,
he has the will to win,
no sport he won't attempt,
nothing he won't join in.

Perhaps to you that's nothing strange.
All boys could do the same,
but it's very different for my son,
when he joins in a game.

For all these sports he loves to do,
he competes in his wheelchair,
a true athlete in his own right,
his joy at winning we all share.

A very normal teenager,
life for him is never dull,
despite a major handicap,
he lives life to the full.

Remember nothing is beyond you,
you must never give up hope,
my son's an inspiration
to those who think they cannot cope.

Pauline Hickey

THE LOST POEM

You were mine!
Conceived in the night, of course,
This morning you called to me
Holding out dimpled arms from the play-pen.

'Just wait,' I said
'While I pay these bills
clean this room
make this phone call -
Now!'
But the play-pen is empty.

Panicking I search and call.
The hidey-holes of my mind
Return an echo.
My affairs are in order
My house is spotless
Without even a snapshot
Of what you were.

My dear, I pray
You have crawled away
To a more loving home
A more caring mother.

Zoë Pearce

VIRTUAL REALITY

So soon the autumn slanting sun
fracturing the memory of June's diamond days.
The body adjusting chameleonlike to these changes
yet the mind clinging stubbornly to that exquisite joy.
What perfect blessings could we store such feelings
to take them out at times
reclothing ourselves in virtual reality.

Joan R Gilmour

BLACK MOUNTAIN WHITE

Sorrow like death's dark breath
Glistens on black onyx faces,
While the diamond eye searches
Through grey wastes of earth.

Peace, touched the universe,
Gathered from the softness of springtime,
Carried on the wings of fine weather
To the mountain peaks.

A damp dark cavern, in the belly of the earth
Where dark shadows crawl, seeking her favoured prize,
Diamond dewdrops, caught in a moment of sunlight,
Splashed from the waterfall sky.

Clamouring sounds,
Heard over heartbeats cry,
Metal on metal, whistle for danger,
Heaving chests sigh.

Hammering heartbeat,
Whistling winds, sortie of sound,
As the mountain stretching
Reaches the sky.

Dark bodies throw salt to the bowels of earth,
Tastes of bitter despondency or candyfloss blossom flow,
Melting into her cavernous mouth,
As earth swallows man and man swallows earth.

Sylvia Shields

GOD'S GARDEN

The views across the countryside
Makes you wonder, with eyes open wide,
Who made this wonderful magic picture,
With which to make our lives, the richer.

Which artist could paint this world so bright
To make every colour and shade, just right,
Just look across those hills and dales,
The beauty of them never pales.

Here we see flowers of every kind,
It really gives us peace of mind,
The detail in the petals prove
They were painted with a heavenly love.

We have beauty all year round
Even in winter, plants abound,
The lovely snowdrop strives for light,
Looking delightful, when it wins its fight.

Then comes the crocus, and daffodil dear,
That's when we know that spring is near,
And in the summer, the splendour of flowers abound,
Now you realise, this must be special ground.

No one on earth could paint like this,
The hand that wields the brush, is His,
People try to copy, and are very good,
But no one can capture, His artistic mood.

Eric Hope

A CHRISTMAS MESSAGE

Christmas wishes to you this day
A time of mangers and bundles of hay.

Glitter, gloss, and smultz abound
Cash tills jar with their sound.

At the end of the day to what does it amount?
The vigorous study of the profits account.

It should be a time to forget trials past
For all to strive for peace to last.

The man next door does not wish to fight
But his leaders, appointed, must show their might.

To love thy neighbour this coming year
Hate, lust, and envy would disappear.

'Impossible for all to honour,' you say,
But it takes only each man's conscience to obey.

To throw off the shackles that bind his mind
Would reveal the compassion for him to find.

If he thought more of love and not drunk with power
The seeds of happiness would burst into flower.

Ah well! 'Fanciful thoughts' you say - I hear,
Let's enjoy Christmas and also New Year.

Peter J Dewhurst

SO IN LOVE WITH YOU

I wake up in the morning
I see you lying at my side
Memories of all the things we did
Last night
My heart beats faster
As I stare at you sleeping
My love for you is so intense
Inside my heart is weeping
I reach out my hand, feeling your soft lips
A tingle runs down to the bottom of my spine
From my fingertips
I suddenly raise my hand
I don't want you to wake
I just need to look at you
Or my heart will surely break
I wonder what you are dreaming of?
Are you thinking of me?
Are you remembering the love we made
So passionately
And then how we lay together
Holding on so tenderly
You are more than a lover
I'll never ever love another
You fulfil every desire, turn a spark into fire
I will always burn, my body will always yearn
You suddenly open your eyes, they shine so bright
Feelings begin to flare, far too strong to fight
Our bodies entwine and slowly become one
Our hearts begin to mould together, from being two
And my heart begins to weep once again
Because I'm so in love with you.

Kate Jones

NO CHANCE

Seal pup trying frantically to find his way down to the sea
He turns and gives a backward glance
He knows he doesn't stand a chance
Man wants the skin upon his back
No mercy's worth the price of that
And as man raises up his club
And brings it down to spill the blood
To run against the turning tide
Another little seal pup died

Patricia Ann Evans

MY LOVE

When it rains, I remember
an aching soul and a crying heart,
standing in pools of the saddest light,
back to back
and moving away - and I knew
the tears in your heart
would soon be on your cheeks
to wet my fingers as I held your face
up to the light,
to remember
for tomorrow.

Whenever the eyes of Heaven overflow
and God's tears wash across my window,
I see again those streaks of love
which flowed for me,
to bind an aching soul
to a crying heart,
and I think of my love.

Chris Hassell

RINGING THE MEMORY

Through the mists of time,
I see the memory in my mind.
I know the day and the date
You were on time and I was late!
You wore black and I wore white
I on the left and you on the right.
We said our vows, proclaimed our love
The vicar blessed it from God above.
And as we walked down the aisle
Knowingly you gave me that fatal smile.
Hand in hand, husband and wife,
Matched together, forever, for life!

Carolyn J Bartlett

THE ARTIST

The artist goes drawing in paradise,
He goes there because it is so peaceful and nice,
A multicoloured parrot flies across the sky,
The artist draws it as it goes by,
He draws the parrot in the air,
As he sketches it down with so much care.

The parrot has flown by as you can't see it in the sky,
He draws the scenery behind it,
Then he takes the paint from the art kit,
The artist paints a palm tree on the sand,
Then he sketches on some surfers in the background.

The artist has drawn the scenery the surfer and the parrot in the air,
Then he draws a tiger that was so rare,
Then he goes back home,
So he can be all alone.

Lee W G T Morgan

SUMMER HIBERNATION

I huddle quiet against the hedge,
Hiding from the world,
Just as the cottages around me
Hide behind their ivy curtains -
Shh-shy in the shrubbery.

The grass around me is tousled by the breeze -
I feel it ruffle my hair.
I am sluggish as the slugs,
Lackadaisical as the daisies,
Shh-shunning sound and activity.

An old man dawdles past on his bike;
His chain watch is for ornament only.
Even the birds protest at the speed of flight,
And settle for hitching rides on the backs of sheep
Shh-shuffling sheepishly through the grass.

In the sky, the clouds ripple lazily,
As if someone had thrown a pebble into its blue:
Sunlight beams translucent through petals,
Behind which screen, the bees are coy -
Shh-shadow dancing to their sleepy drone.

Honeysuckle in the hedgerows is heady . . .
I feel myself succumb,
And rest my head on a carpet of celandines,
Glossy under the hawthorn, while the sun
Shh-shines silkily through thistledown.

I snore to the rhythm of the church bells,
Which toll, muffled and apologetic;
And sleep through the passage of time,
marked by floating dandelion clocks -
Shh-ships of filigree cradled by a barely moving stream.

Sandra Lloyd-Jones

THE SUN

Silence drifts along on the wind,
Minutes pass.
My mind is keen as I feel for you.
I search everywhere,
You are not among the clouds
Nor the trees
Nor the flowers
Nor the grass.
Hours pass.
I feel your presence near
So I turn.
Your reflection is in the water,
You smile,
I dip my hands into the stream
And try to catch you,
But your reflection breaks
Into a hundred thousand pieces
And you fall
Back into the murky waters.
I cry
Tears of loneliness.
You must be somewhere
Anywhere,
Everywhere,
Nowhere.
You've slipped away
As silently as you came.

Sophie Bennett (Age 15)

THE ROBIN

I knelt at the foot of my dear Saviour's cross
and my heart was heaving with shame
I wanted to tell Him how sorry I was
to have caused him such sorrow and pain
But the words that I uttered were lost in the air;
my Lord was so far from me,
How I wished I had wings, and could share in His grief
as He hung on that cold bitter tree.

Just at that moment a little brown bird
flew down to answer my prayer
And I whispered 'dear little bird
please help me to tell Him I care.'
His little head bowed for a second or two,
and all was quiet and still
And then again he was lost to me,
as he flew to the top of the hill.

He circled around that cold sorry place
then perched on the dear pierced brow
He sang his sweet song in the Lord's sacred ear
and I knew my message was heard.
For he looked down on me
in pity and love
and I felt just one Holy tear.

The little brown bird stayed there with his Lord
to comfort and sing his sweet song
And then with his breast stained red with His blood,
he lifted his wings and was gone.

And now when the skies are dark overhead
and all is stark and drear
I think once again of my dear feathered friend -
his song once again I hear.

That sweet little robin so much wiser than I
who is bound to this earth with feet made of clay
yet he to the Heavens can fly.

Gladys Locke

THE DIETICIAN

Who are these people
Who write book after book
On what we should eat,
And how we should look?
Were they called names
Just like one of us,
Fatty, or thunderthighs,
Or back end of a bus?
Do they eat lettuce
For meal after meal?
I say they should try it
To know how we feel.
I'd like to believe
That they have flab too.
Do they have problems
And do they feel blue?
Why should everyone
Take a size eight?
And who says what
Is an ideal weight?
I look at their books
And see a new diet.
When next week comes
I think I'll just try it.

J Owen

COUNTRYSIDE CURES

The open air, the meadows where
I often go to think
Breathing deeply, mind completely
Empty, so I drink
The heady smells from flower bells
And sink, and sink, and sink . . .

Drifting away beyond the day
I float upon a cloud
Of fantasy, no one but me
Wrapped in nature's shroud
Of grasses tall, a lush green wall;
Heads serenely bowed.

The sun is warm upon my arm
Over which the beetles crawl,
Birds start singing, voices ringing;
With each harmonious call
Their lullabies weigh down my eyes,
As I absorb it all.

My mind is full of sun and soil,
Life's worries slip away.
A butterfly goes flitting by
The rabbits, as they play
Among tree stumps; then one thumps,
As the buzzard seeks its prey.

The sun goes down, its golden crown
Giving way to night;
So I must go, contented now
My troubles seem so light.
It's good to know whenever I'm low,
Nature will put things right.

Sapphire Zagni

REDEC OF KEIRON

In Kieron the king called for music - a child was born.
Only a girl, but healthy, a sign of better things,
and besides, she had the king's mother's eyes.
But the music was poor, the players nervy and shrill,
and childbed fever burned through the queen like fire,
while the child lay silent, listening in her cot.
The queen died, and the king's favourite horseboy
ran off with the flautist, and the king's favourite horse.
So they named the child Redec, which means trouble.

The king wed again and in time there were sons,
weak mewling things, while the girl grew straight and tall,
all bones and flying limbs, and the king's mother's eyes.
The old men in their hovels shook their heads,
and land was sold cheap for gold, and the new queen ailed and died.

The king wed again, but on his wedding night,
his long-dead mother watched him from the dark
and he left his bride alone to giggle with her maids.
As the boys grew weaker, suitors came, weighing a sharp-tongued wife
against a throne - she laughed at them with the king's mother's eyes
and they left - a poor kingdom anyway.

Then came a prince of sorts, three windswept farms and a well,
but bold in his ambitions, and the boys were dying now.
So Redec sought the seeing-pool and asked, what shall I do?
What can you do, the dead women sighed, and she thought of her mother,
weeping and dying alone, while the music played
and on her wedding night she took a kitchen knife
thin and sharp and killed him where he lay.

They burned her as a witch, as painful a death as childbirth,
but her own choice, and that night the dead women watched
as the king lay sleepless, and high on the hills above Keiron,
the wolves wait.

Janet Smith

EVERY MEMORY

Frozen in time
Lifeless
A lowly hourglass
Deprived
Of all motion
Those shifting sands
Silent
As whispering thunder
And love's dying moments
Captured forever
In a photograph
One of so few
Staring back at me
As I flick through
The pages of time
A solitary tear
Regenerates a feeling
In grief I remember
Things
I had taken for granted
Every tear's a memory
And every memory cherished

S Meredith

CHOPPER

I see you nineties bird of prey
hovering over the motorway,
your aviation fuel kerosene
mixing below with gasoline.

Choking field mice and darting voles
killing badgers and velvet moles,
ensuring another sad demise
of regal birds, once ruled the skies.

So there run the mechanical mice,
there is no doubt we'll pay the price,
they can run but they cannot hide,
at the end of their costly ride.

Another colossal human
blunder, and failed attempt to steal
God's thunder.

David Robinson

PEACE

The tragic, bloody war rages.
Families in poverty, cold, starving
and nowhere to live.
The sound of destruction. The smell
of rotting, the sight of buildings alight,
fire blazing thick black smoke,
The drone of aircraft going to fight for their
burning, nearly destroyed country.

People weep for their loss of family
rubble and bombed buildings
Germany's destruction had ruled people's lives
The sheer terror terrifies all
But the spirit of bravery keeps them fighting
The spirit keeps saying, 'We'll win this awful war!'

Years after the ghastly war-fields of blood red poppies
mark the battlefields.
The blood of honour has sunk into the ground.
The beautiful flowers mark their heroism, friendship and teamwork.
The lucky and fearless survivors may have lost their friends and
family, but not hope!

Thomas Lynch (10)

HOME AGAIN

I returned to the valleys, driving slowly up the vales
I just couldn't believe my eyes, what has happened to Wales?
I stopped the car, looked around, at a sight never before seen,
Turned left, right, up and down everywhere was green.
I blinked, rubbed my eyes, then looked once again
No pit or tip, grime or dust, I must be going insane.
Checking the sign, yes it was the right place
The filth and muck had vanished, not a single trace
I thank God He remembered this wonderful land
And decided to give mother nature a hand.
Oh no, what a pity, here comes the rain
Some things never change, I'm back home again.

J P Williams

FIELDS OF TRANQUILLITY

Such mysterious wonders lie amongst, fields of tranquillity.
A time to be reminiscent,
A time to be lost, within the thoughts of your mind.
As you close your eyes, you fall under the skies,
You are subdued by the calm and warming atmosphere.
You lie upon angelic ground,
Gentility and purity surrounds you,
A world of peace and innocence.
Sweet breezes roam the air,
You have no knowledge of time and life,
Only your deepest imagination lives.
You see only beauty,
You feel only warmth,
You smell only sweetness,
As you listen to the gentle ripples of a flowing river,
A completion of celestial enjoyment,
As you lie amongst, fields of tranquillity.

A R Rankin

HOME

Alone in the cold in the wind and the dark,
Sleeping alone in a lonely car park,
Drugs are your comfort as you lay there alone,
No hope for tomorrow no place to call home.

You're desperate and dirty alone on the street,
Begging for money from the strangers you meet,
Sometimes you wonder where food will come from,
Alone and rejected no place to call home.

The drugs get a hold and they won't let you go,
You're looking for something but what you don't know,
You fight to survive you moan and you groan,
But you're still in the gutter no place to call home.

Then one windy night when you're full of despair,
You try something new and you utter a prayer,
Then an answer comes to you from God on His throne,
I hear you my child I'll give you a home.

You then start rejoicing your life starts to change,
You don't understand it in fact it's quite strange,
You're not on the streets now just left there to roam,
For Jesus has saved you, you've now got a home.

One word to encourage you people out there,
Alone on the street in utter despair,
The answer's so simple and to you must be shown,
Jesus is waiting to give you a home.

David Paul Lloyd

STARLINGS

Scoot
Ritzy misters
natty dressers
city slickers
Jack the Rippers
filchers grabbers
swagger swaggers
dance hall strutters
slick Mick Jaggers
hell raisers
gate crashers
safe in numbers.

Glitz and glamour
file and hammer
tooth and nail boys
out on bail boys
mouth and trousers
railing raiding.

Bright and easy
sleekly greedy
no-one's darlings
laméd starlings
rash brash dashers
fruity looters
root toot tooters
Scoot.

Marilyn Gunn

DOLOROUS

Her body is a derelict structure,
And she's set in neglected ways.
With the filth of cold street doorways,
Cloaked in a drunken haze.

There's no beauty in her lifestyle,
But she doesn't seem to care,
As for the parasites who bleed her,
She is totally unaware.

Christmas is a time for shivering,
Searching for a dry place to stay.
While summer comes to take a coat off,
And keep her warm the easy way.

And who's to tell the reason why,
She walks the vagrant's track,
And who amongst you sitting,
Will lend a hand to bring her back.

And who amongst you really care,
Whether she will live or die.
And at her graveside would there be,
A heart that would truly cry.

Is there one who instead of forgetting,
Would chance to send a rose.
Or shall she pass unnoticed with,
Her pile of cast-off clothes.

A E Graham

THE SNOW AND YOU

It snowed the day after you were born
It was April after all
And I was drunk so late that night
That I missed this rare snowfall
Hours before I'd heard your cry
I'd seen you change from blue
Into the right thing for us both
Into all that is you
I staggered round the house
Remembering all that had just been
A solo celebration for all the things
I had just seen
But I really did so little
While you two had worked all day
And had to have another to remind me
It was okay
Early hours Saturday, new-born
My whole world white
I slept it off
So proud to be a father overnight.

James Bull

LET IT BE SOON

Let it be soon,
Have peace in our land,
No more wars, lay down our arms.

Let it be soon.

Animals in danger, on land and in water,
Let us protect them.

Let it be soon.

Our sons and our daughters
Will bring love amongst us.

Let it be soon.

Give them the strength
To believe in oneself.

    Let it be soon.

Yvonne Edwards

SOLDIER BOY

The beaches of Dunkirk are never at rest,
Soldiers who died there were amongst the best.
Letters they sent home to wives, sons, daughters,
They spoke of the trenches, deep in mud,
Swamps, and dreadful stenches.
Lord, they found the burden of war hard to carry.
To all British mothers.
All our soldier lads are our sons,
We admire them all and love every one.
As I kneel in the village churchyard, by my soldier boy's grave,
My eyes fill with tears for his life he gave.
I was a young girl then, when this war was on,
Now all these lonely years since I kissed you, have now passed on.

There is not only one hero in war,
Many thousands have marched on before.
Many poppies have grown upon your grave,
Reminding us of the lives our soldier boys gave.
And I just want to say, I still love you my hero,
In remembrance we honour, all lives that were lost.
Red on the poppy reminds us of the blood that was shed,
Black in the middle, tells us to respect the dead.

Marie Graha

MY BOSS

My boss just gets right up my nose
With everything he says and does
He cannot lead or motivate
Direct, plan or co-ordinate
With every word he loses grip
He can't control this little ship
To sum it up, he's pretty dim.
Should you run a management course
And need a case study, use my boss
His lack of skill is second to none
We'll work much better when he's gone.

Veronica Summers

SPACEMAN

If I could be another I wonder who I'd be,
Would I be someone famous, or a nonentity?
Perhaps I'd be a spaceman and walk among the stars,
And stand and look back down to earth from galaxies afar.
I'd be up early in the day to dress in special clothes
With tubes and wires everywhere and a helmet over my nose.
I'd reach the spaceship check it out, prepare to blast aloft,
Then settle back until I reached the blackness deep and soft.
I'd steer the spaceship past the moon, and past the morning star,
Continue past planets like Venus and red Mars.
And then I'd reach the galaxies of which I'd often dreamed,
Then spend the day chasing meteors as onwards they all stream.
Perhaps I'd meet others in different sorts of ships,
With different shapes and languages before I'd homeward slip.
I'd land the ship back down on earth and quickly walk away,
And wish I'd had the courage to land up there and stay.

Winifred Jenkins

MIRROR, MIRROR

My mirror told me
a thing or two today,
it directed my eyes
to deepening lines
and additional grey.

We didn't argue or
disagree, but decided
not to see each other
as often as we used to.

Avoiding a scene, off
I go to reflect on other
things; it just hangs there
and never changes.

James Sherman

SURVIVING

Hungry people, no money, no home,
Nowhere to turn to, on the streets they roam,
Begging and stealing, it turns into crime,
When you have nothing, there's no sense of time.

Neglected, no shelter, nobody cares,
Sadness and suffering, no love to share,
Sleeping rough in doorways and lanes,
Who do we punish, who do we blame?

There are just so many, it's hard to ignore,
Surviving all odds, as a means to being poor,
How did it happen, what did they do wrong?
All they wanted was a meal, somewhere to belong.

Dianne Brown

TINKERS

Not poets please! I beg! That's far too grand for us.
Not wordsmiths - though, that is within our radius.

Tinkers rather. For we take word-coins and rub them in the dirt
And shine them with its earthy power to make them bright and pert
And solder them together in ways not done before
So each one lights another's fire and they all glow the more.
And sometimes hammer them a bit (but gently, hand of mine!)
And dress and drill their syllables and push them into line
But so the whole should never pall and make the reader bored
We may leave one out of line. Naughty word!

We rake discarded lexicons for tired, worn-out words
Like philomel and amaranth and gossamer and sherds.
We try to give them all new life that they may once again
Be breathtaking, and crystalline, in language's domain.
We oftimes heighten meaning where the older one's forgot -
Is 'a sherd of dreaming' nothing but a bit of broken pot?

Our aim is to communicate and never be obscure
And use those tinkered syllables in ways serene; ensure
That readers pick them up and stow them in a place
Where they fill a tiny empty well; illuminate a space.

And sometime, I hope many times, we tinkers may aspire
To fashion from a bunch of words we shined up in the mire
A quiver full of arrows, straight as light and light as air:
Arrows very nearly painless - you will hardly know they're there
But they'll pierce your street-wise armour be it made of what alloy
And they'll prick the very soul of you and make it bleed for joy

Tony Jennett

CARDIFF

Cardiff has changed so much, you can see,
Modern buildings and shopping malls, burger bars,
And all the trappings of modern times,
But the older generation, such as me,
Like to remember Cardiff just as it used to be.

Queen Street - the old Dutch cafe,
The Kardoma, the aroma of fresh coffee filling the air,
The hustle and bustle of people rushing everywhere,
The old trolley buses whizzing by,
Old friends waving as they caught each other's eyes.

The old arcades a shopper's paradise,
Large old imposing buildings lining the narrow street,
The old milk bar, now they have turned it into a large Boots store,
Most of the old shops replaced,
It's a very modern city now.

But thank goodness, some things will never change,
The castle and the City Hall still stands for all to see,
The museum, one of the largest in Wales,
Now that's a place that could tell many old tales,
The fountain built to honour the Prince of Wales,
The tiny park filled with beautiful flowers,
Where visitors spend many happy hours.

The old city is now the capital of Wales,
We are proud of it of that there is no doubt,
But just sometimes I wish they hadn't messed it about,
I realise that we have to move with the times,
But it's nice sometimes to keep the old memories in our minds.

Terri Brant

PLEASE MISS

Will you help me to be a writer like you
To show people pictures without a camera
To take people to faraway places without leaving your home
To keep the very best of all, that tells of life
That stands time's longest test
And that, for all to know is the written word
And that's the best

The boy stood on the star ship's deck
Wondering what his future held
Now his heart was filled with pain
Blaming himself for what never came
Yet his smile was filled with hope

Cut backs to the left of me
Cut backs to the right of me
Into the valley of cut backs rode the disabled hundreds
Ours is not to ask this government why
Ours is to be quiet, suffer the stigma of the disabled, then die

To be a painter of pictures
Not with the brush, but with the pen
To open up your imagination to the very wonders
That the biggest and best motion picture soon ever invented can show

The word is the picture of the mind
The heart is the cinema of the soul
Write well, oh writer of words
So that you can show me the very best pictures

James Thomas Hopkins

A CRY FOR LOVE

In a crowded room
of cots and beds,
Left alone -
With no mum, so soon.

She struggled to her legs to stand,
And for attention, she would demand.
But no one came near,
So she cried aloud with fear.

Now this she did on every day of every week,
As she was only a baby still,
And could not speak.

Her home was an orphanage
run by nuns.
She had the loudest cry,
And would hold her head high,
over the cot,
hoping not to be forgot.

A nun would nurse her,
And prayed for a mother
To come and love her.

The crying stopped
When that prayer came true.
Thank you . . .

Janet Marian Burns

THE AWAKENING

One day, when all was quiet, as I reflected on my life,
My thoughts were full of melancholy, misery and strife,
I considered my position, wishing that I could be rich,
Envying those more prosperous - my despair reached fever-pitch,
My career had no prospects, and growing older day by day,
I became sadder by the moment all my mind in disarray,
As I walked along the byway with a slow and heavy tread,
I was filled with such foreboding - I viewed the future with much dread,
Then I chanced upon a vagrant, with broken shoes and threadbare socks,
Newspapers for his blankets in his makeshift cardboard box,
Nearby I saw a blind man, seemingly at peace,
Yet confined to a world of darkness, from which there's no release,
I reconsidered my position - I had much more than wealth,
I was blessed with friends and family, and the gift of robust health,
My fortune may be meagre, and my ambitions won't come true,
But somehow, the air seemed sweeter, and the sky a brighter blue,
As my thoughts grew clearer, I could see the way ahead,
My step became much lighter, now that my fears had fled,
I felt happy and contented, and I know the reason why,
The assets I already have - money could not buy.

Our Bri

COMING HOME

Why does the journey seem so long?
I'm in a hurry you see,
It's been a long time since I was home,
The place I yearn to be.

I was happy enough while I was away,
But what of the feeling inside?
It's something I find rather hard to describe,
A feeling I could not hide.

Good friends, I made, I felt at ease,
But that little something was missing,
My inner self was saying 'Please,
Take me where your heart's wishing!'

Yes, there's one thing I've learned from life,
That no matter where I roam,
Though I can be happy somewhere else,
There's nothing like coming home!

Pamela Williams

BROTHER

He stood there dressed all in grey
  With a hymn book in his hands
As he lifted his head with tears in his eyes
  Singing oh for the wings of a dove.

We sat there in silence my mum and I
  So proud of what he had sung
A tear trickled down his cheek
  As my mother whispered that's my son.

There were many there that Christmastime
  to share their happiness
Giving presents and joy to all their boys
  And warm feelings of tenderness.

I'll never forget that special time
  For as long as I shall live
Seeing my brother after many years
  Gave me one big happy thrill.

Even though he looked happy on the outside
  I know he was hurting within
For many many years later
  He committed suicide. A sin.

J E Hill

TO A SLUG

Of nature's bad excrescences
You slippery, slimy slob
Attacking all my lettuces
Their sweet young leaves to rob

To look at you makes me feel sick
Your feel makes me throw up
Your slimy chilliness is quick
To stop me picking up

Your filthy fest'ring flabby flesh
(If worthy of that name)
Please don't attack more of my fresh
Seeds in my new cold frame.

Slivering, slippery, slimy slug
Sheltering in my shed,
Eating all my seedlings . . .
How I wish that you were dead.

But I don't know your family,
Your wife waits your return
To help her make new little slugs
That is your main concern.

Slinky, slimy, sleazy slug
Don't make me want to kill you
Get out of here, leave me alone
Let other people fill you

With *their* sweet vegetable leaves
Their super succulence
So go to try what *they* have grown
Through the garden fence.

Maxwell Bruce

A DAY IN THE LIFE OF MR MELLOW INGRAM

I'd had a very weird dream
I believed I was Elvis
I awoke at the crack of sparrows and ran to the mirror
Like me old, this Elvis was old and bald
The facial features were there
And wow when I opened my mouth
What a voice!

The plan, look through the papers
I figured I could do four karaokes and a talent show
Tomorrow who knows I could be
First things first visited the chemist
For some Gary Glitter face cream
The ageless look, a bit of black dye
For the thinning hair, yeah I was there.

Well I got some of that no it can't be looks
Now so convincing I had my lunch and beer free
Dressed up blew my top, first show knocked them down
So good they followed my to the second
And free beefburgers.
The word was around, everyone thought I was real
      I was.

I waggled, I shaked, Elvis Pelvis was this
How they screamed, the band played good
Hot sweaty crowd, the flashlights spotlights
      Tonight is good!

It came to midnight, the stage hit me with a thud
I awoke Mr Mellow Ingram instead
With a hospital full of roses at my bed.

Aled Hughes

JACK FROST

Does he exist?
Finding in the morning
the window panes engraved
in exquisite patterns of ferns
each one perfect
as they are when they grow

Jack Frost is secretive
He does not wish his existence to be know
He knew I had found him
The next day the pictures had changed
Exquisite detail again
but different patterns of leaves

If there was central heating
and double glazing
I would not have seen this miracle
It is believing in fairies
and Father Christmas
I would like a scientific explanation

K King

MEN MUST NOT CRY

The chapel was full, like never before,
They crammed inside and looked at the floor,
Of course, you know the reason why,
Because in our culture, men must not cry.

Oh, they can laugh, and joke and swear,
And drink and fight and dye their hair,
And though I know no reason why,
It seems, it's wrong for men to cry.

But a friend had gone for ever that day,
And though there are lots of words we could say.
Nothing could change the unfair fact
That a man had gone, and couldn't come back.

And the women could sit and the women could sob,
They knew him as neighbours, or through his job,
And the men could shake their heads and sigh,
But that is all . . . for men must not cry.

Thomas Phelps

FEBRUARY

Grey the sky, grey the sea, grey the colour seems to be
The winter month of February.
But, if only one would look around, a wealth of colour can be found.
For a tapestry of colour is on display in the park, on a February day.
Fairy-like snowdrops clad in white - fill the senses with delight.
Crocuses so vivid and gay - purple and yellow they display.
Star-like primroses so shy, on mossy banks of green do lie.
And the tender buds of the willow tree, are such an enchanting sight to see
In their soft fur coats, so snug and warm - safe from the frost and winter storm.
Daffodils in gowns of gold - beautiful and bold.
On banks and hills and under trees, abundantly they grow.
Squirrels on a distant bank - scurrying to and fro
Searching for their winter store, they hid months ago.
A robin in his bright red vest, perches on a tree at rest,
Watching all who passes by, with his bright and twinkling eye.
Black and white magpies on the wing - what a raucous song they sing.
Glossy blackbirds with yellow bills - so sweetly do they sing
Accompanied by the gurgling stream,
Reminds one of the spring.
Grey the sky, grey the sea.
Grey's not the colour of February.

Sylvia Bevan

EVALUATING ENVY

The town dweller envies the countryman,
in his white rose-covered cottage,
The struggling slimmer, her seven-stone friend,
who devours egg chips beans and sausage!
Harassed mum envies her briefcase carrying friends,
and her power-suited ultra-glamorous sister,
While she in turn has envied her two kids, nice house,
and being married to her perfect loyal Mister,
Lonely Princes in their castles,
envy their subjects' normal life,
and Joe Bloggs would change with him,
just for no money worries, and maybe a tiara for the wife.
Pop stars in their electronic prisons,
envy those who don't have to cope with fame,
and thousands of future 'wannabees'
just dream of being household names.
So envy no-one anything,
what is meant for you will surely be,
As often envy can lead to the other sin,
which is greed and gluttony.

Joy Marles-Roberts

VALLEY OF A THOUSAND STARS

I fell in love with a thousand stars
As they looked down o'er the place I love,
Winking and twinkling, like a thousand eyes
They lighted the valley from up above.

I saw in the moonlight, shining bright
The homesteads dotted here and there,
Sending a glow of cosiness
As I breathed in the fragrant nectar air.

And as I wandered the Celtic glen
Roaming to Llan and back again,
I knew my heart would know no peace
'Til I dwelt in the Vale of Ffestiniog.

Monica Mary Jackson

LIFE JACKET

My life is a little worn
and frayed at the edges,
limp around my shoulders
and soiled with the fingerprints
of those who tried to touch me up
but had no flair for fashion.

I want someone to seize my life
and turn it inside-out,
tie-dye it,
scrawl words of pride down each lapel
in thick black
indelible ink,
sprinkle it with spangles and sequins,
then spin me round six time to see how it fits.

Stylish, I'm sure.
Haute-couture, even.
Watch
me cartwheel
down
the
catwalk
once more.

Susan Richardson

THEY DIDN'T UNDERSTAND

Born into a world that did not understand.
It never would, it didn't want to.
He wasn't the first and he wouldn't be the last.
But still they did not understand.

The kids in school teased him, he wasn't like them.
They called him names, they stole his lunch,
And they kicked him every day.
They just didn't understand.

His mother yelled, and his father hit him.
He was their failure that would never go away.
He cried.
They did not understand.

The man at the Jobcentre said: 'I'm sorry we just can't help you.'
So he tried to help himself.
But time after time they turned him away.
They didn't understand.

His parents both died, leaving him all alone.
Nobody helped, nobody cared.
He was a problem.
A problem they did not understand.

The streets became his home.
The bins, his source of food.
His prayer every night was always the same:
'Please God let me die, they don't understand.'

His heart was filled with sadness, his eyes filled with tears,
When he took his own life.
It was his only way.
For the last words he mumbled were:
'Maybe now they'll understand.'

Tracy Wheeler

US

'About suffering they were never
Wrong, Old Masters.' Before 'The Plaza
In the corner of the room'
Tragedy confronts us universal
Pictures, as Commodity insists
A soul-destroying time.

It's Bosnia now, slimy rag-dolls
They drag from earth to show us.
Their loved ones, sweet sorrowing they cry
The camera's regurgitating image
Spouts spools, post-haste to comfort
Chairs and apathetic eyes.

Do we all turn away leisurely
From disaster? Or recall for
Effect at social tête-à-têtes?
Or ease our conscience with our prayers,
Or money? How can we ever learn?
Or is it far too late?

Or should we open up our veins
And let them flow? Like One, they
Say, who died two thousand years ago.
Or should we open up our veins
To let them know, how deep our
Heartfelt love and sympathy *could* go?

'Weak fools' they'd say,
Few men are sympathetic
Anyway. But we must have
Learned something? Maybe true.
'The loving that only
Loving brings.' We send to you.

Sonia Ruckley

CHOCOLATE CAKE

Your face seems to melt
In the gas light glow
Shining and waxy
Your features slide
Unrecognisably downwards.

As you speak
The words leer over me
Poisoning me
With their finality.

On the matted rug
Beside us
A carefully prepared sweet
Sits squat
Running, glistening
In full view of the furnace.

Karen Taylor

GREEN GRASS

I begin to forget
the smell of the grass,
when I wondered if you'd ask.

The summer eve
and a trace of dew,
and the trail to find a place.

It is long ago,
and I'm 65,
- it's further and further away -

But the *new* young feel,
and it's still the same
in the warmth - oh the smell of the grass!

Mags Middleton

VARIEGATION

Our lives are a world of variegation,
A kaleidoscope of pigmentation.
Spectrum, polychrome, spottiness, tessellation,
Zebra, chameleon, batik, maculation.
Stripe, streak, dot, bespot,
Speck, fleck, plaid, peacock.

If we lived a monochrome life,
Neutral, drab, dingy and grey
What a sombre, melancholy existence,
Despondent, gloomy not dulcet and gay.

Jane Cook

SECRET AS THE POLLEN

waterfall and river flow,
cloud over hill
what do they tell:

      love is . . . settled
as the sky - sky-surf
rolling and breaking high above the Bluff:

      love is . . . silent
as the plainsong of the adam-appled Wye
rousing the pebbled bed at Hay:

      love is . . . simple
as the dimpled fold of Clyro Hill,
flower and stamen and fertile soil:

secret as the pollen
that waits in the bell
of the purple campion as it blows in Offa's Vale.

Angela Morton

TOY SOLDIER

The little boy plays well into the night
Positioning his toy soldiers for their next big fight.
Airfix models strategically placed
Cannons pointed at each other they're faced.
Meccano constructions, books galore
have all been removed from his battle ground floor.
The Army and the Air Force, he is so keen
Just peep through his door, it's a sight to be seen.
The little boy lost in his land of battlefields
moves his best soldiers behind a tank for them to shield.
He was such a happy, carefree typical boy
Playing for hours mapping out his next ploy.
The boy one day becomes a man
Changing the battlefield of his next game plan.
The battlefield and game plan so far removed
from the littered bedroom in which he once stood.
My 'little boy' often thinks of his land faraway
Sparing a thought for us 'live soldiers' as he goes through the day.
His days filled with teaching children, but his mind he lets roam
He thinks of his bunker, the one he calls 'home'.
Maybe the weekend, he thinks to himself
The plans he's already made, he'll put on the shelf.
He will set off to see the 'squadron' he thinks
Once there, he'll go with the 'General' for a couple of drinks.
He'll be given a good dinner by me, the 'Chief in Command',
Then he'll wander upstairs to the room where his wars were planned.
There are no more 'toy soldiers' now, to march on their bellies
Only a stereo, computer, video and telly.
Please 'little boy' come out and play
Come home forever to us and stay.

Karren D Kinsey

MANHATTAN'S LEGACY

We didn't laugh,
we didn't cry,
we didn't dance under crimson skies.
With bleeding hearts we watched the dawn
of that final day when the sky was torn
from the Earth's embrace; when my father died,
his molten face
screaming a final farewell.

We couldn't breathe,
we couldn't run,
no longer could we see the sun.
I called and cried for my mother's arms,
(that fond embrace that heals the harms
of a cruel world), as the cloud unfurled,
its burning rain
drowning a stricken land.

We can't forgive,
we can't forget;
our foes will someday pay their debt.
With subtle hands we'll mould mankind
to a way of life that rots the mind.
Will you have fun as the rising sun
controls
where once it screamed?

Ceri Vale

THE GREAT MYSTERY

His pain is palpable.
Desire to know so strong
It envelopes the heavens.
An all-consuming need
So strong it burns into his very core.
A constant ache in his soul.
The depths within him
Unfathomable.
The need makes his being
Shake with frustration and aggression.
Every cell seems to throb.
His brain is heavy - tired,
His eyes dry.
Yet;
The answer
Is as much a mystery
As the reason for looking for it.
Why do we live?
Develop
Become educated,
Make ourselves lives we love,
Then die?
We will never find an answer.
No matter how you think.
Philosophise,
The great mystery will always confront you.
Life.
He is every man.
Enjoy.
Don't think.

Rhiannon F Hart

COVETOUSNESS

The bourgeois Luke has Jesus say
In the Sermon on the Plain,
'Blessed are the poor. For they
Are spared much angst and pain.'
But the nouveau poor Saint Matthew writes
'Blessed are the poor in spirit,'
And the grateful Tories think he meant
That all their wealth is heaven sent,
Only it mustn't make them cocky
Like the greedy, selfish Labour mockers.
Yet Matthew gave up his hoarded gold
After he joined the Christian fold,
While Luke, the bourgeois who liked his brass,
Remained a child of the middle class.
Matthew no doubt began life poor
Until his job have him wealth galore.
Was he an hypocrite? Was Luke sincere?
Matthew should bless those who have no money,
Luke should have blessed the poor in heart.
Luke was a bourgeois - that is clear -
Who beats Matthew hands down when he writes to be funny,
But is sometimes too learned to speak from the heart.
A pink socialist safe in his bourgeois job
He loved to bless the penniless mob.
But Matthew stresses in his screed
That when wealth corrupts, its cruellest art
Is to fill our hearts with corrupting greed.
That is what Matthew learnt to his cost
Before Jesus found His sheep that was lost!

Peter Gledhill

CREATURE COMFORTS

Now I'm old, now I'm weary,
Life is all but done.
Here I sit in gratitude,
Looking back on years that have gone.

No regrets mar my pleasure,
The inward eye is calm indeed.
And like most my age,
Creature comforts are all I need.

Once I was a handsome fellow,
Proud, as any given birth.
Mine was humble, but no matter,
In my home I ruled the earth.

My life has been happy,
Though blows came thick and fast.
Still in sanguinity,
I knew they were not meant to last.

Now I feel that I am ready,
All I want is to say goodbye.
And go to meet my maker,
Up there in the sky.

Margaret Cave

EMPTINESS

Never touching
Never knowing
Never asking why
Never thinking
Never caring
No more tears to cry

Always wanting
Always hiding
Always running away
Always hoping
Always wishing
I had something left to say

J Hatton

JOKING APART

A silent ocean of stagnated slush,
Mummified beings, set in the gel of time,
Oozing - fermenting,
Waiting.

I tread with precision - afraid of movement,
The earth, petrified by environmental waste,
can no longer turn,
A sphere,
broken.

Breathing laboured - I perspire with fear,
Alien sounds, reaching my brain,
Eyes pierce the horizon,
Danger ahead,
death.

I gather up my children,
after, yet another hot, sticky day
at the beach.

Sue Whiting

MY BABY BOY

I have a beautiful baby boy
Who brings me a lot of joy
Tending to his every need
Every morning make his feed
Splash-splash in the bath
Atishoo-atishoo it makes him laugh
Lying fast asleep in his cot
After playing with the toys he's got
A shelf full of cuddly teddies
It takes ages to get him ready
Everyone says he seems to happy
But doesn't like me changing his nappy
In his way he tries to talk
He loves going out for a walk
In the clinic to be weighed too.
Even more washing I have to do
I've no more time for gardening
He crawls about into everything
He's almost one year old
And worth more than his weight in gold
I'm his mother and I love him so
Would I be without him? *No.*

K Brown

THE BRITISH LEGION OUTING

To wait in line to board the double decker,
Food and coins held tight in sticky hands,
Meant winter dreaming realised
And time again to play on summer sands.

Close-packed we'd sit upon the Newport transport.
Smiling if we'd won the highest seat.
Laughing at the way our aunts and mothers
Sat wilting in the scorching summer's heat.

Watching dads and uncles pack the crates in cars.
The loading eased with many willing hands.
The beer would travel faster than the buses
And be opened when we got to Barry's sands.

A day to spend on paddling, digging, racing,
Donkey rides and eating sandy food.
Losing shoes and coins and sometimes children.
Then funfair time for all not just the good.

Now homing dark has come unbidden.
We busward go with flossed and toffeed hands,
To sleep on corporation buses
And dream of next year's trip to summer's sands.

Jane Wallis Hicks

BREATHING LAST OF THE ONCE MADE (NOW HISTORY)

something
intentionally
eventually
inhaling
breathing last of the once made now history
exhaling
breathing out what was
a million years before
a million years after
here I stand now
so remember the top line somehow
slowly drifting from made beginning
day to day memory sweat
only living for a sample
only living to forget
here I am with this ageing aura
I remember I was once a child
growing forward into the future of no return
too late to be redesigned
yesterday's skin has shed its duty
tomorrow's skin is on the other side
in between fading memories
trying till the end of reality
wanting to go more forward
but stained on rewind
too ignorant to admit time passes whilst river flows
every step counted for
either one step in front
or far away back
and two steps below -

P J Thomas

FRUSTRATED PSYCHOPATHS?

One shot! Two shots! They breed one another
Each target becomes the same as the other.
The world of field-sportsmen who enjoy taking life,
killing the defenceless whom they know cannot fight.
They wield their cruel weapons without fear of restraint,
like 'pit-bull' fight followers, are they just inadequate?

For they breed birds just to shoot, and foxes to hunt down.
Happily slaughter badgers, indeed anything on the ground.
With new genetic theories on behaviour patterns from hell,
Will they use them as a reason to hunt humans as well.
The hordes of frustrated psychopaths could make it their aim
with no shots returned at them, they kill without shame.

Life to these people except if it's their own,
Seems of little value where guns rule the show.
Man hunts through his instincts they will have us believe.
Yet put them in danger, you will soon hear them squeal.
In mind, are they just throw-backs from Prehistoric times?
Little advanced mentally from the old Stone-age tribes.

Tribes who at least killed to survive and to eat,
unlike the 'modern hunter' to whom killing's a treat.
Think when hearing reasons for this slaughter called sport,
When criticism and legislation are merely a joke.
When next you view nature in its design and grand plan
Would you agree its one failure was the creation of Man?

Graham Griffiths

WONDERFUL

Miles apart, they drifted away,
to visit other places,
not seen before.
She blesses the day she met him,
and their destinies remain undetermined.

They always searched for silence,
in a world full of open cries,
not heard before.
He remembers the day he met her,
and his future lies undisturbed.

They are two, yet spiritually undivided,
flowering with every season,
not seen before.
She discovers every part of him,
and yet their souls remain pure.

They danced beneath a thousand moonlights,
two precious silhouettes,
parading through the midsummer breeze.
He protects her from tomorrow,
and they narrow the distance.

M J Kavanagh

BUBBLES

Life is like bubbles, rainbow coloured;
watery skin, and they burst.
They sail upwards, wavering slightly
as if they'll float forever
and they burst.

Bubbles of dreams, new ventures
and creativity, and they burst.
Bubbles full of excitement and zest
for life. Happily ever after bubbles . . .
and they burst.

Blowing bubbles, shaping like life;
round bubbles, slightly out of shape bubbles,
fragile as life itself bubbles, and they burst.
Rainbow bubbles fading as they float,
ascending, until they burst.

Bubbles of life, bubbles of dreams,
bubbles of new plans and schemes.
Bubbles of affection, love and ecstasy,
rising, never to come down to earth.
They rise and pop in mid-air.

Sue Davidson

THE SIMPLE THINGS

The things we take for granted,
the things we get for free.
The flowers from seeds we planted,
are there for all to see.

The early morning sunrise.
A rainbow after rain.
Seeing multi-coloured butterflies,
as we stroll down a country lane.

Young lambs in the fields at springtime
swans gliding gracefully upon the lake
young birds that sing in the springtime,
that we hear, as we become awake.

Night skies lit up by moonlight,
with a backcloth of twinkling stars.
The calm of an evening twilight.
Can all this be truly ours?

All the beauty that surrounds us.
Things to see of an everyday.
The many sounds there are around us,
like the laughter of children at play.

So many special happenings,
that each, in turn, we all share.
How much would we miss ;the simple things,
if they were never there?

Ken Bruford

SITE FOR DEVELOPMENT

Fallen into disrepair
Overgrown and broken
Windows smashed and tiles are down
All testify unspoken
A place that once was cleaned with care
Now finds its day are numbered
They'll knock it down and start again
With site that's unencumbered
A modern structure will arise
With technical construction
What cost this modern excellence
- It's character destruction.

Andrew Hodson

SONNET OF SLEEPERS

A gruelling wind sweeping across headstones
Blows without lenience adding to anguish.
Old iron vases spoiled by age remain
Unfilled, lacking the colour of lost years
When flowers abundant hinted at hope.
Ragged greenery devoid of feeling
Cannot console as well as loving hands
Which once tenderly cared for every grave.
Ensuring beauty and silence to sleep
For those who had been summoned to lie there.
Now the sleepers beside the stone building
Avoid the knowledge that money means more.
No more sleepers or headstones will join them
In Loving Memory replaced by 'For Sale'.

Sarah Jane Davies

NOW, OF A SUMMER EVENING

At a crossing
One January night
In frosted silence
I knew my brittleness
Enfolded in lifeless sky.

When the train came
I watched yellow-lit comfort
Slide by.
For a moment
I was cradled by thoughts
Of upholstered warmth.

Bereaved by its passing
I searched the air-waves
Tuning to the warmth
Of radio chatter.
Bland, brief friendships.

Sometimes in the summer
After our evening meal
I walk among tall grasses
To the centre
Of our sun-warmed meadow
And look back for comfort
To see early evening light
So that I can feel again
The cold edge of loneliness.

Andrew Sumner

AFTER ALL

After all is said and done
You know you were the only one
The one so close in thought and deed
Answering my every need.

After all the time that's passed
You know the truth, I know, at last.
I'm sorry for the wasted years
And all the times that end in tears.

After all, I promised you,
And always meant to remain true
And in my fashion so I did
And in your way you understood.

After all, we slipped apart:
I never meant to break your heart
And when you said to go: just to leave,
What could I do except believe?

But after all the years away
I always dreamed about the day
When quite by chance our paths might cross
And you'd forgive the pain of loss.

After all, some dreams come true
But I was not a dream to you
But cold reality: and pain
And you won't let it hurt again.

After all the time it took to heal
Your pain, you never want to feel
Again the hurt of being in thrall
And you don't want me after all.

G Headley

INFORMATION

We hope you have enjoyed reading this book - and that you will continue to enjoy it in the coming years.

If you like reading and writing poetry drop us a line, or give us a call, and we'll send you a free information pack.

Write to

> Poetry Now Information
> 1-2 Wainman Road
> Woodston
> Peterborough
> PE2 7BU